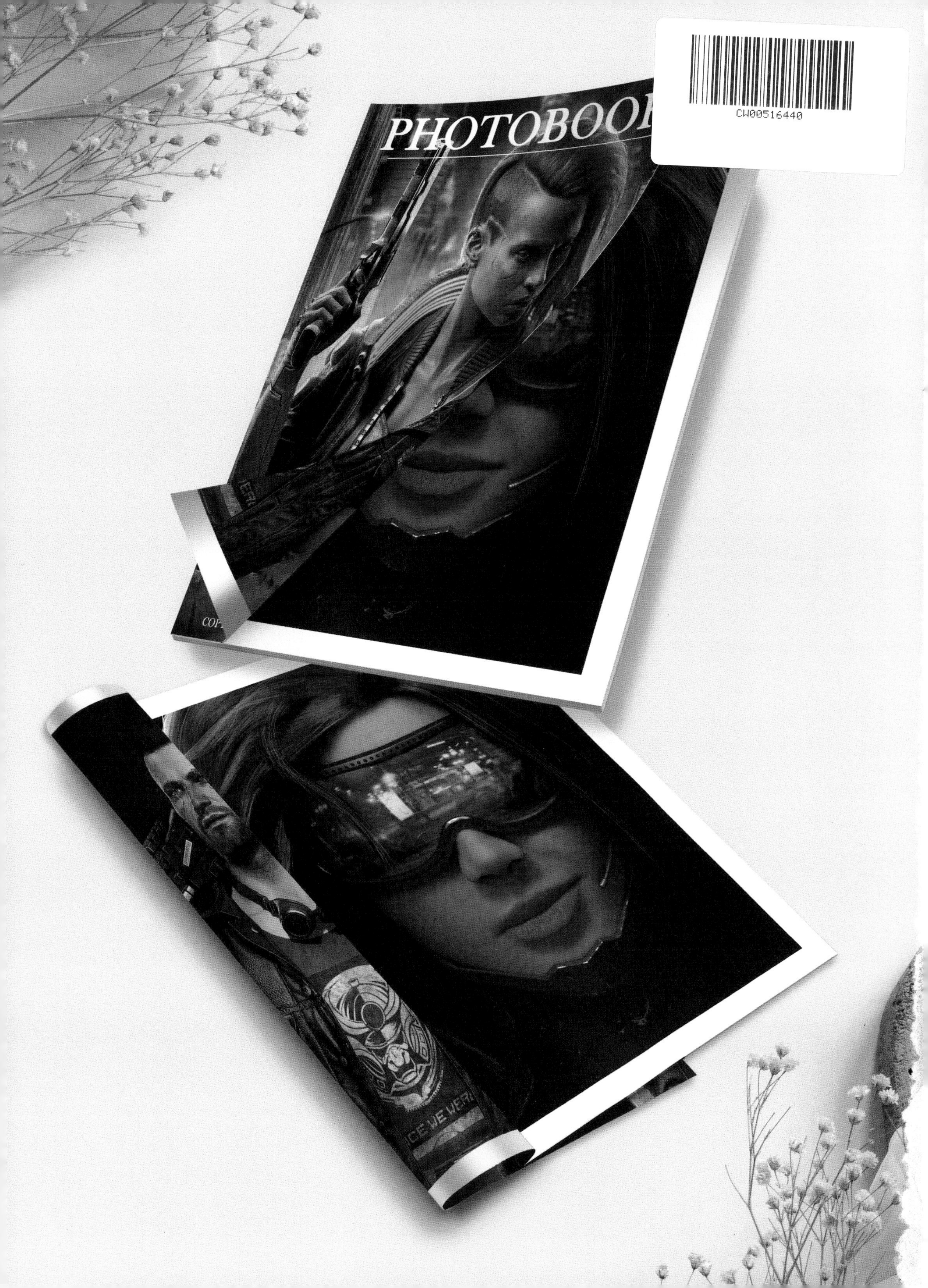
PHOTOBOOK

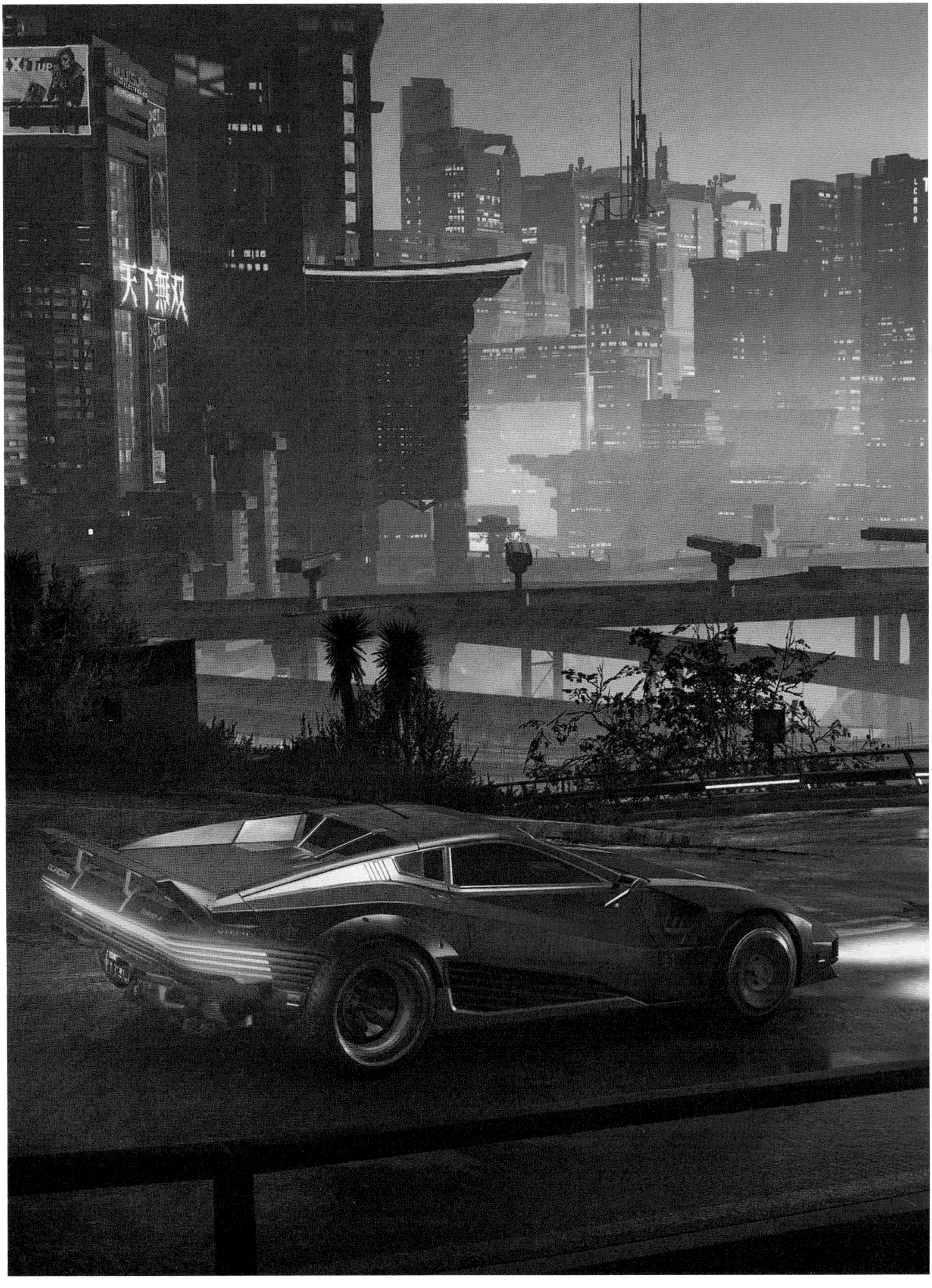
天下無双

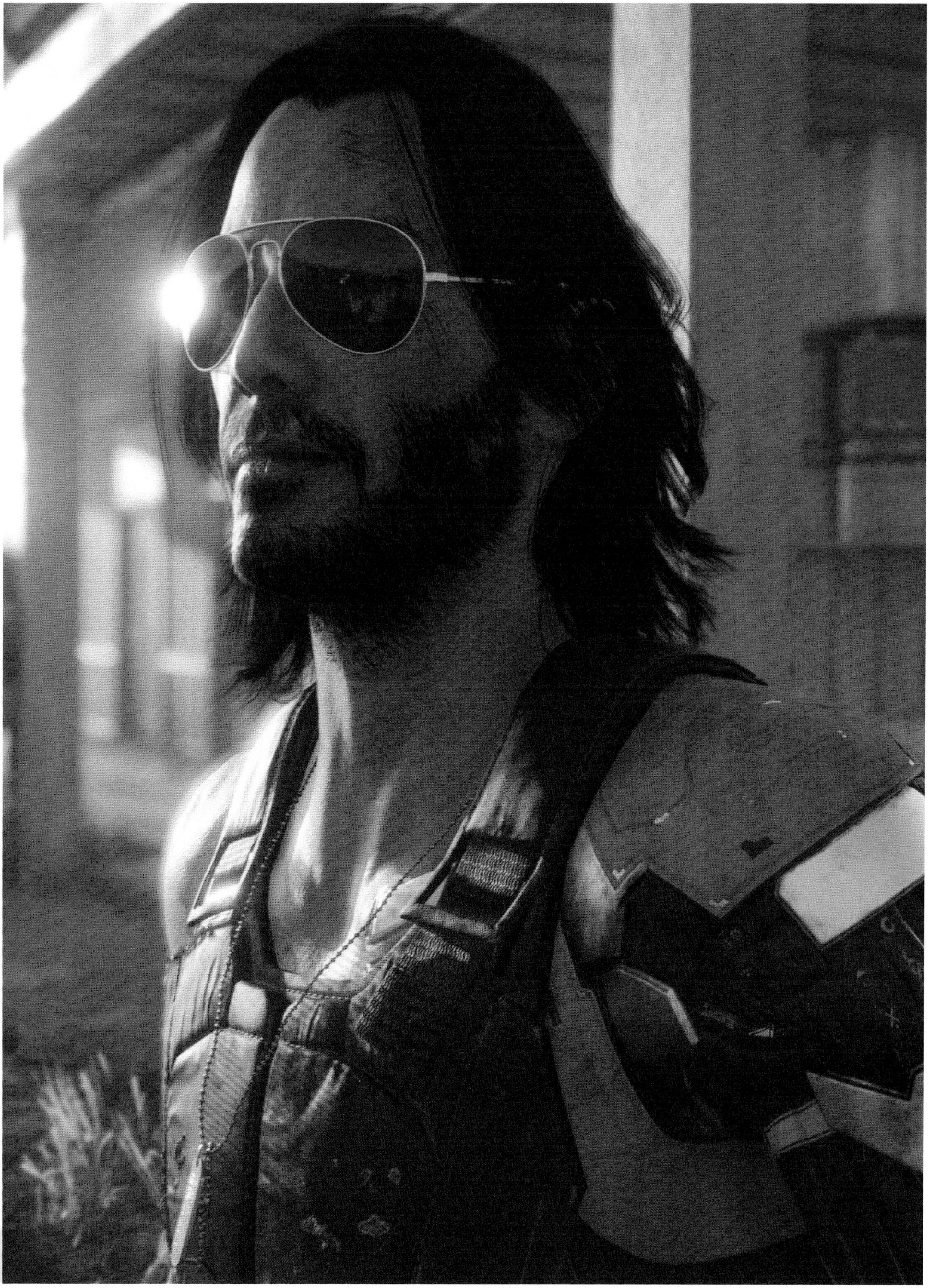

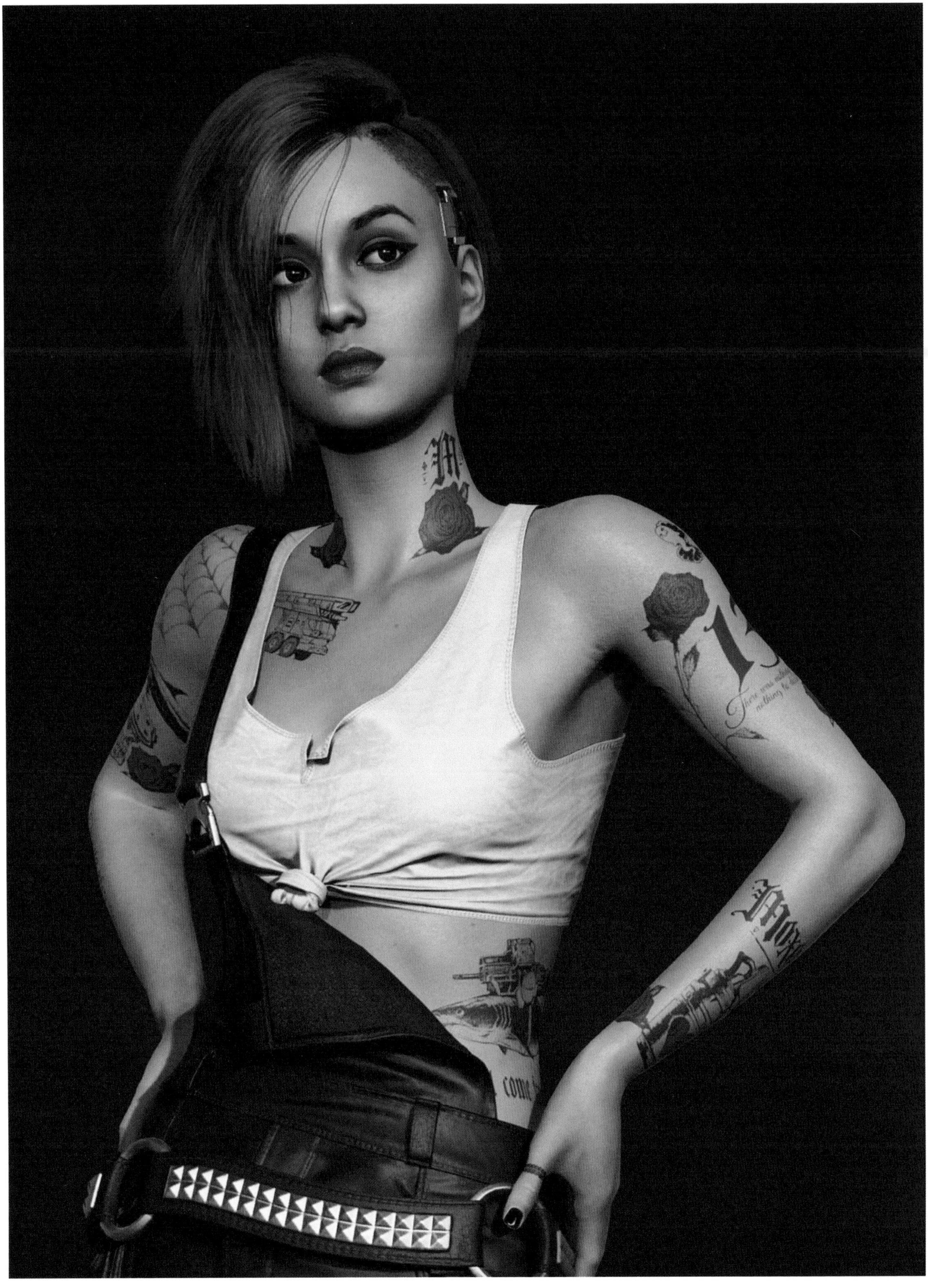

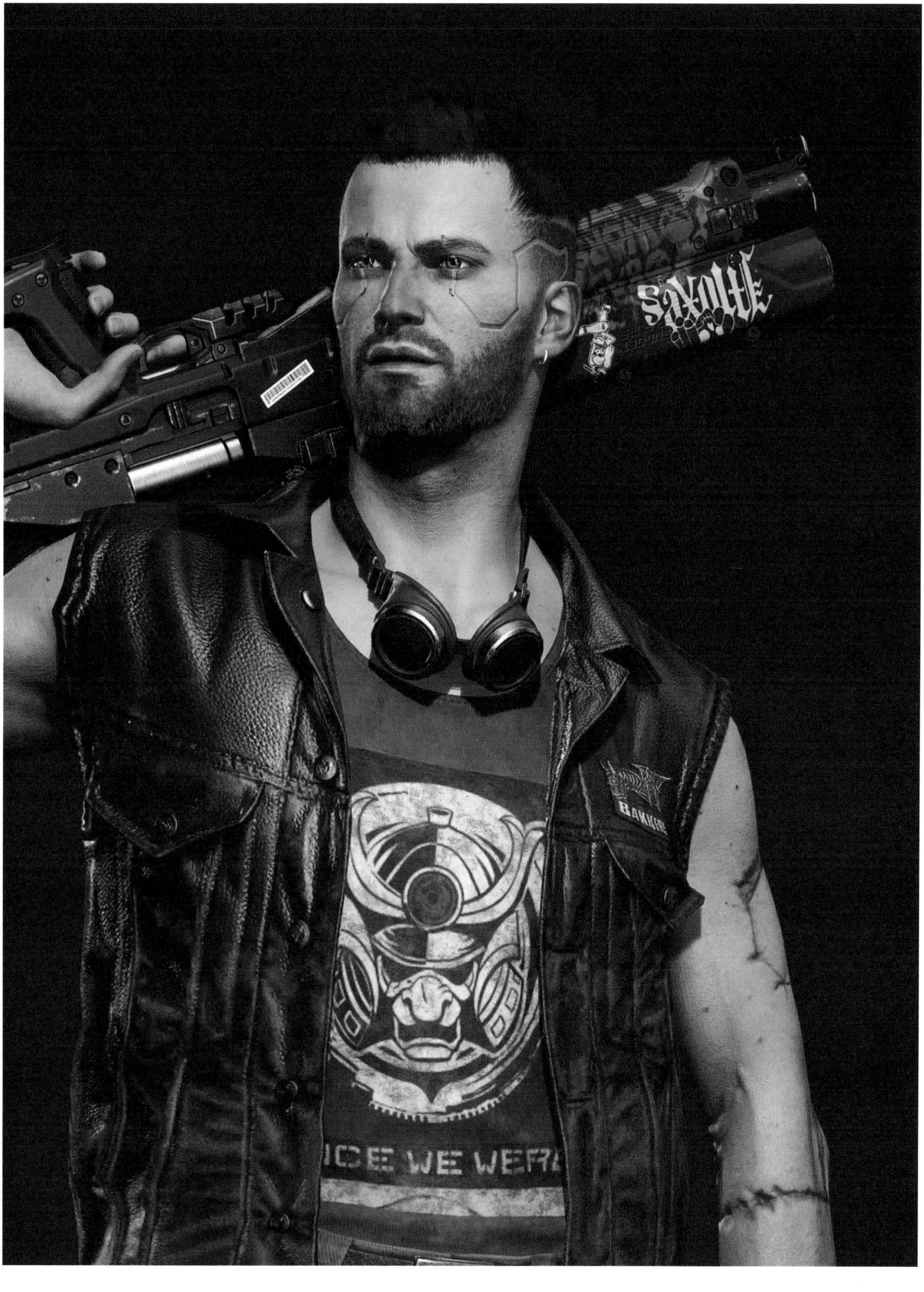

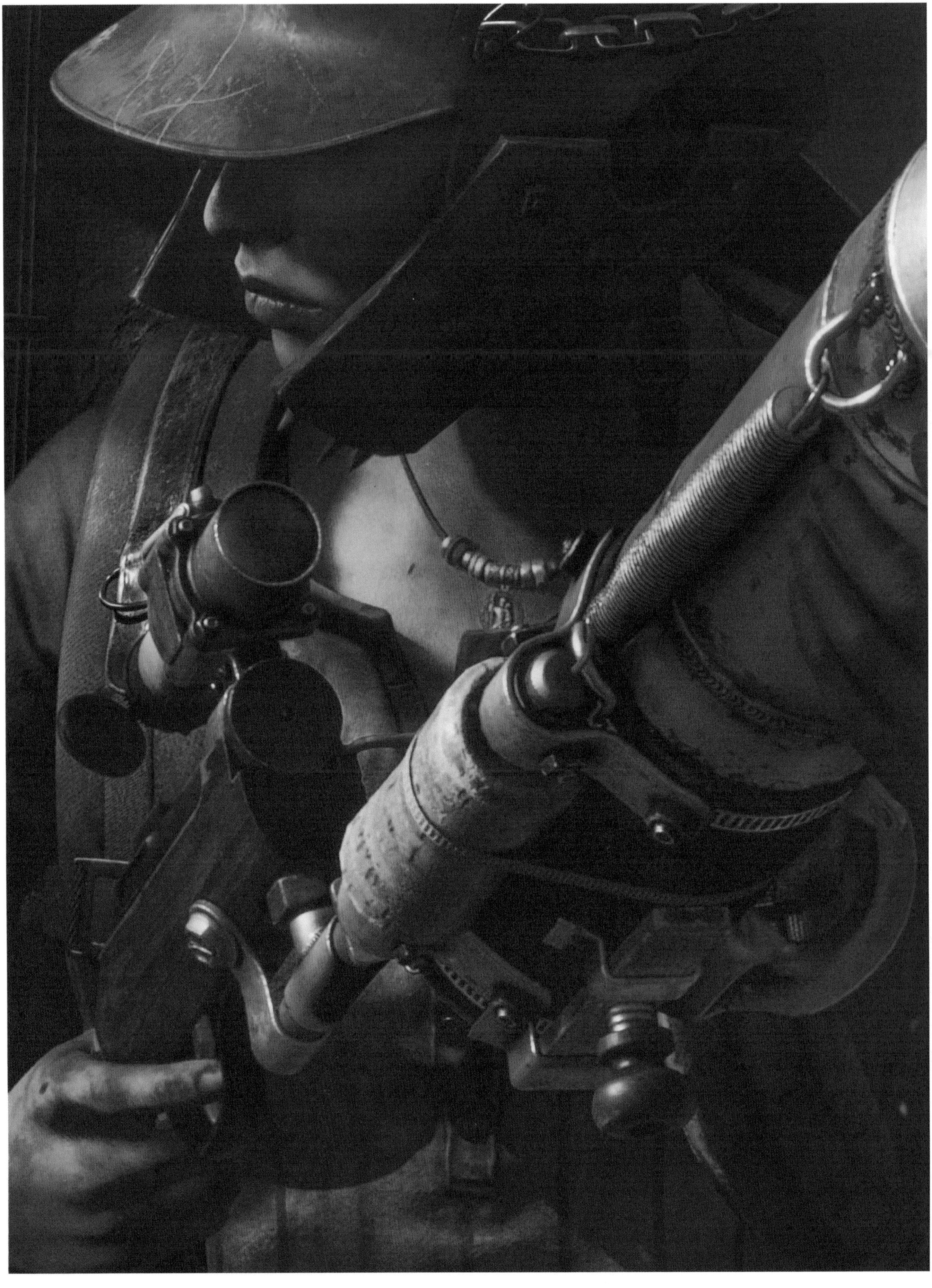

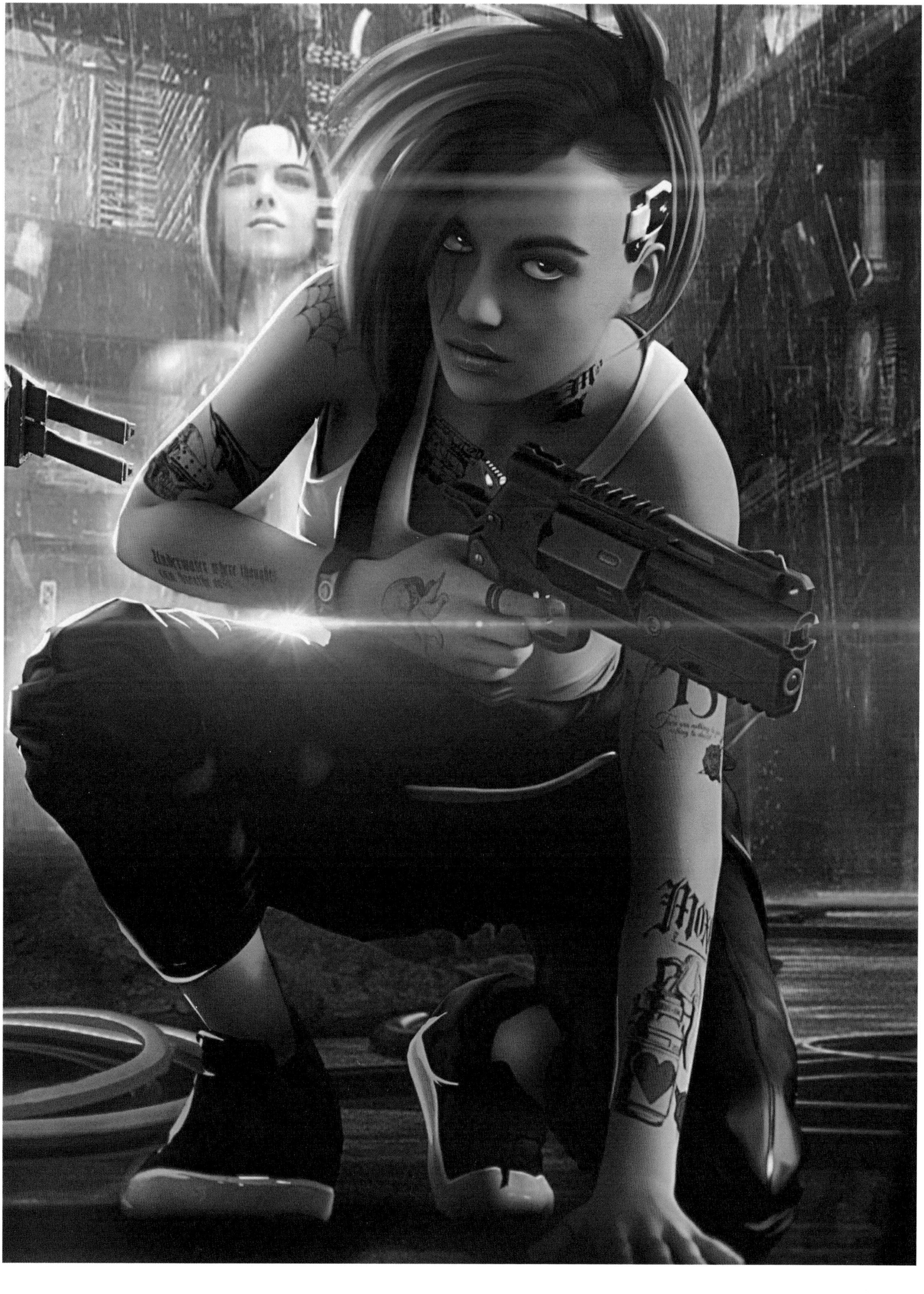

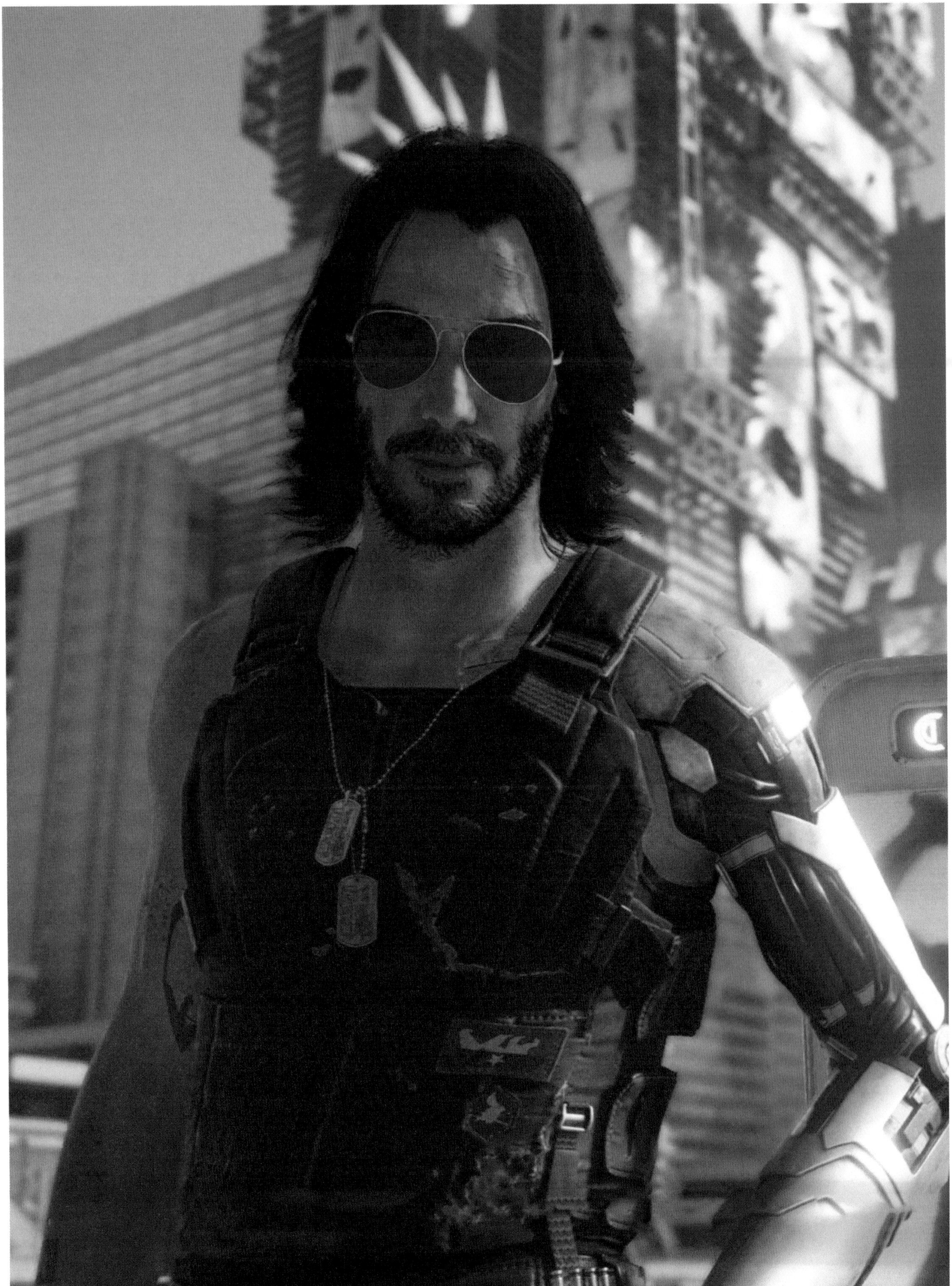

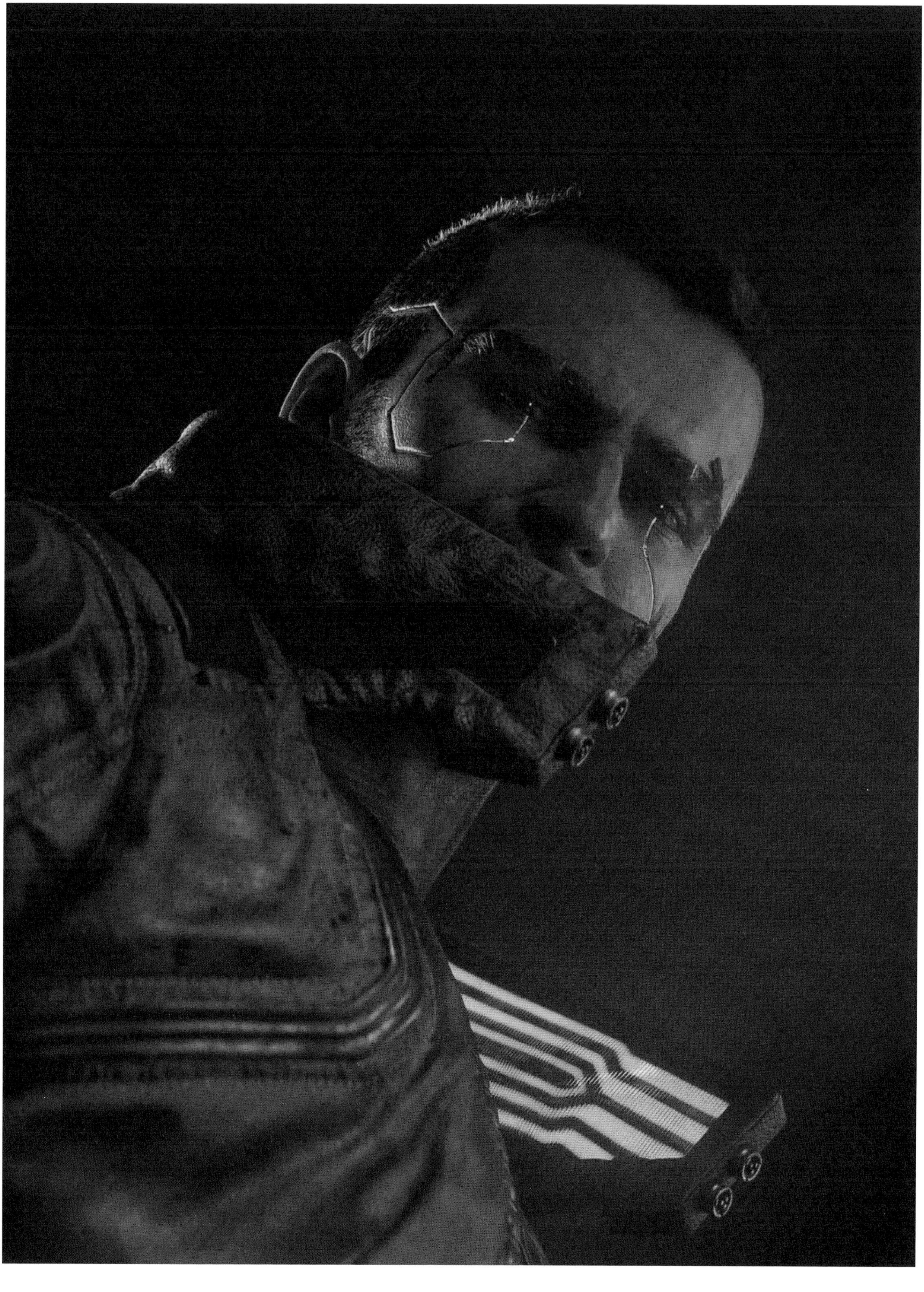

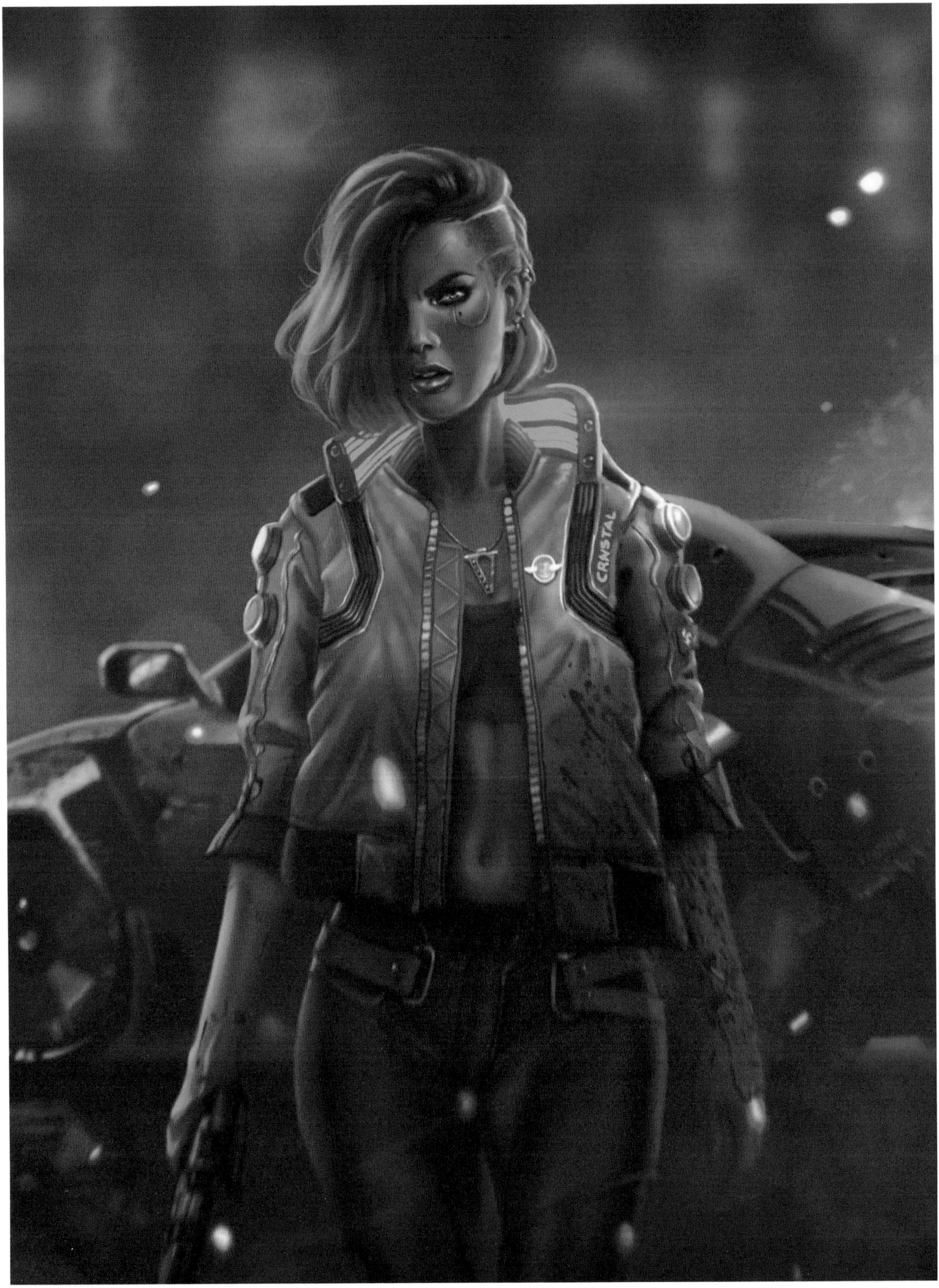

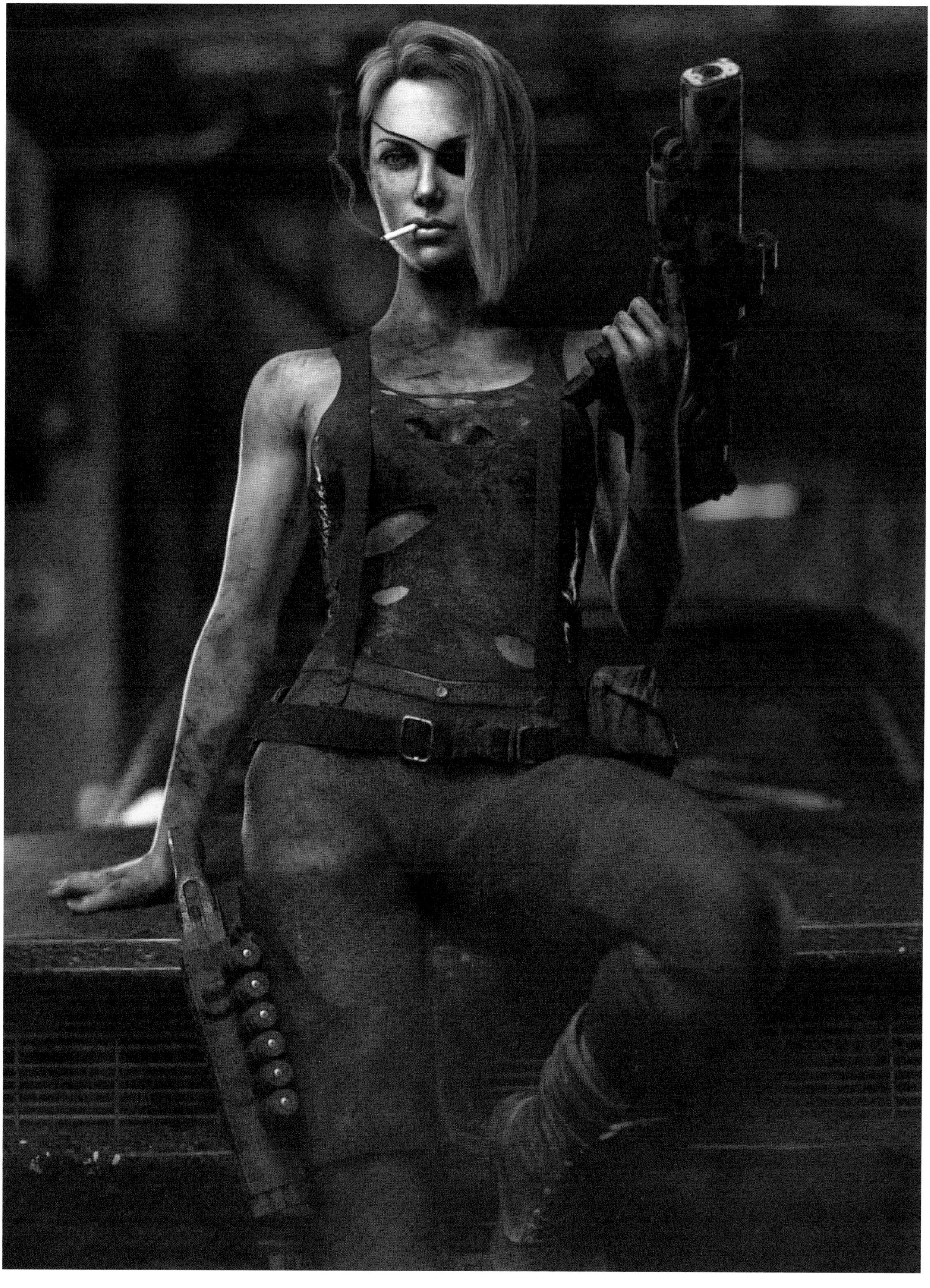

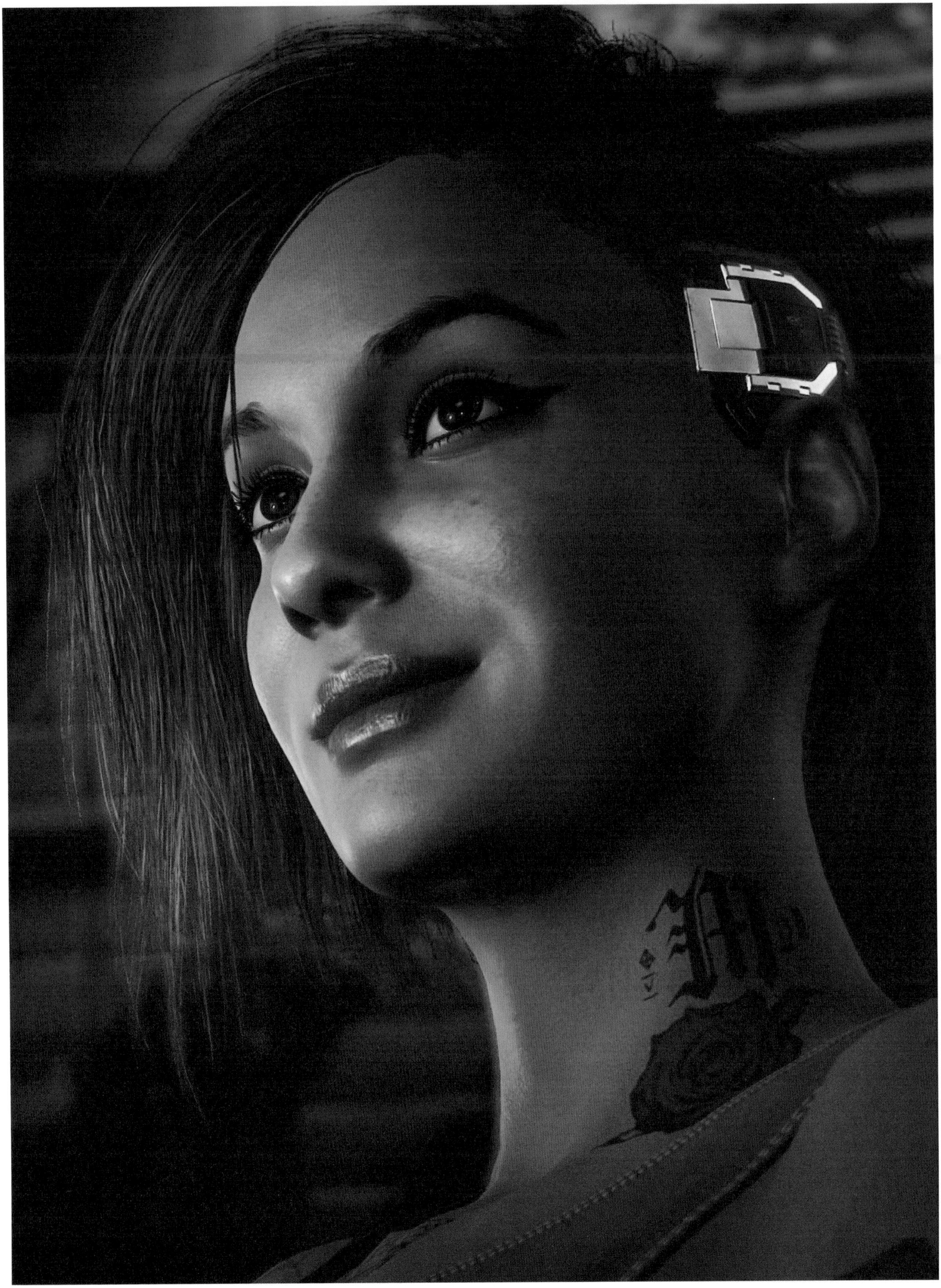

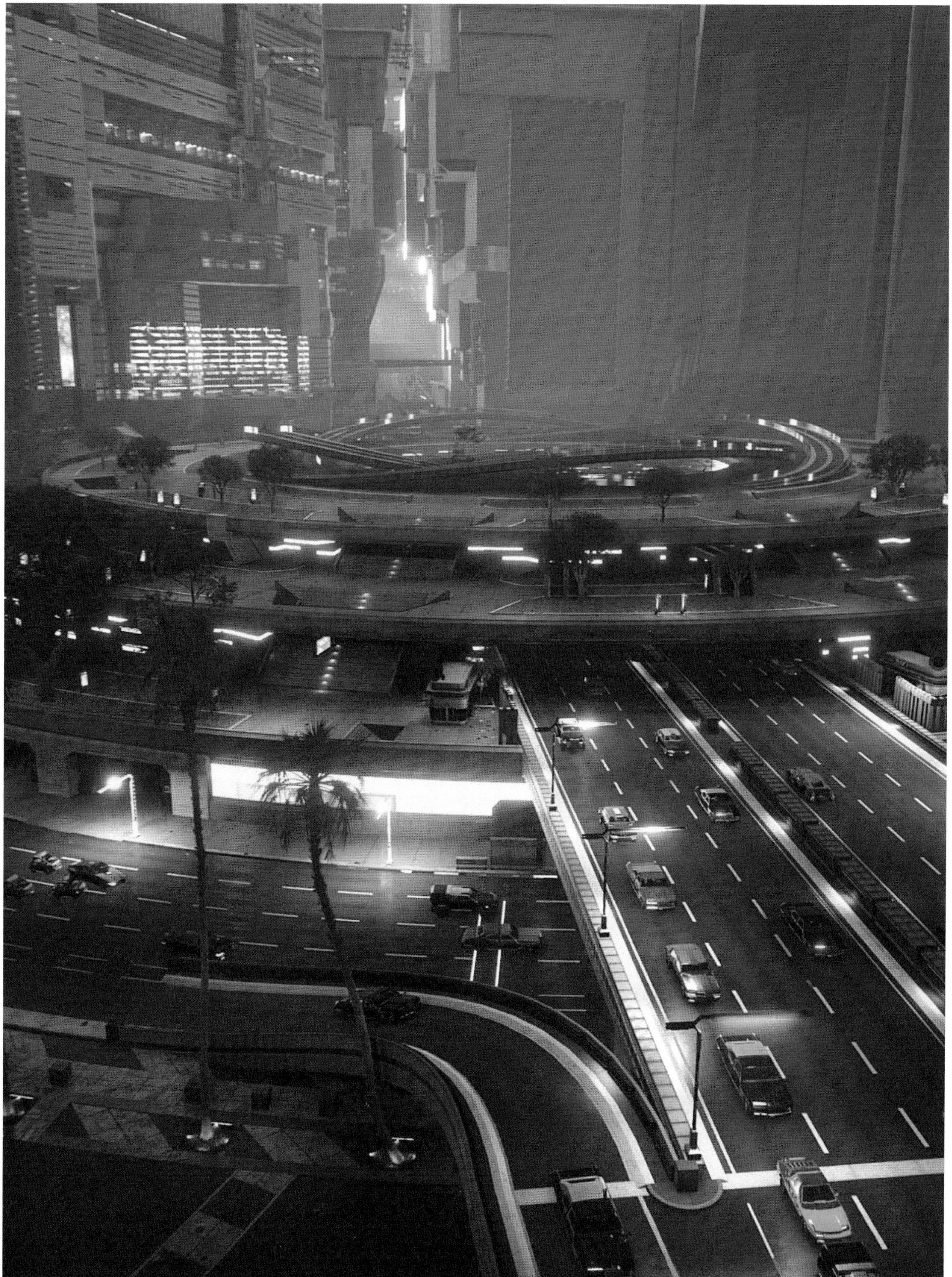

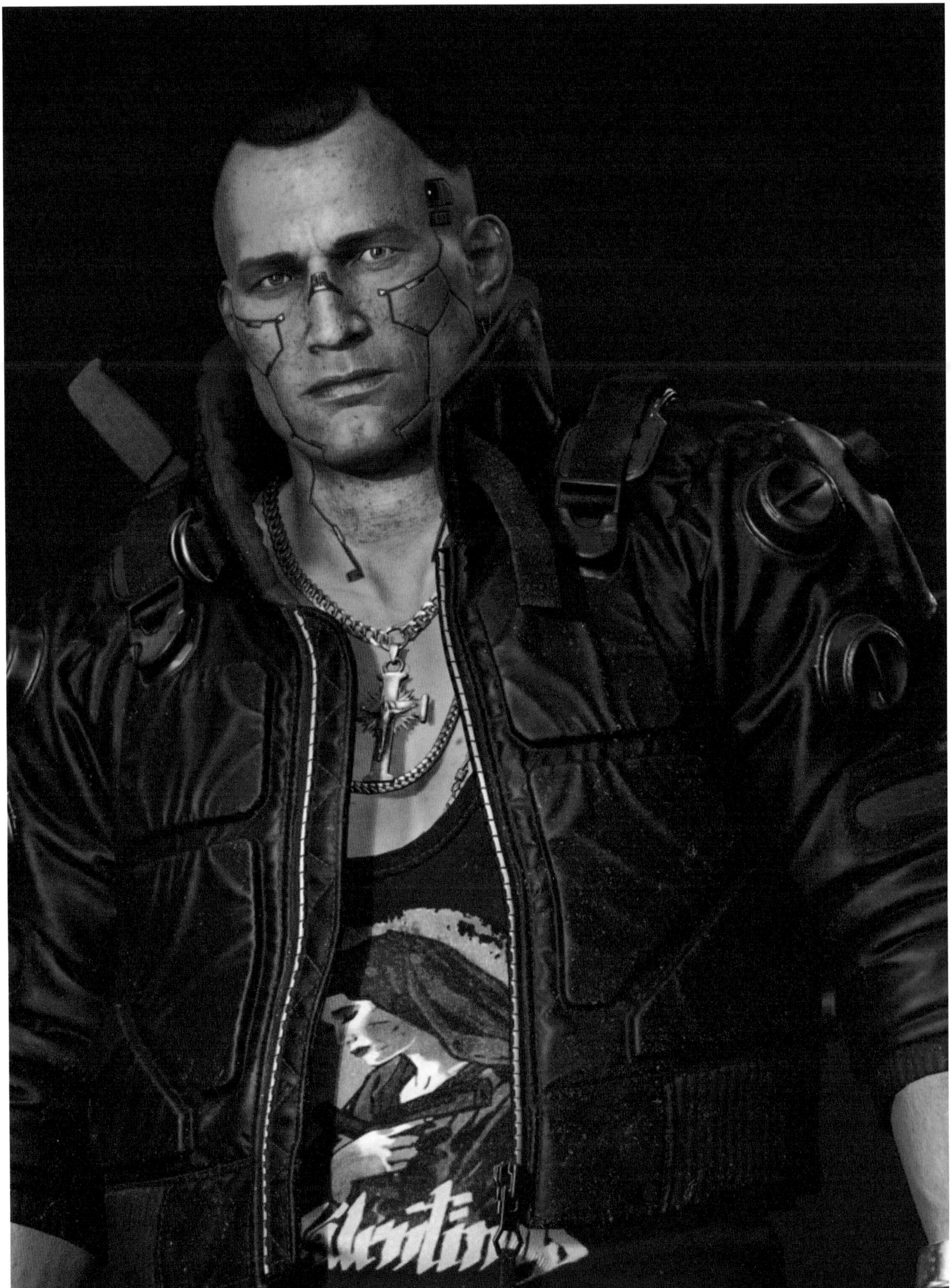

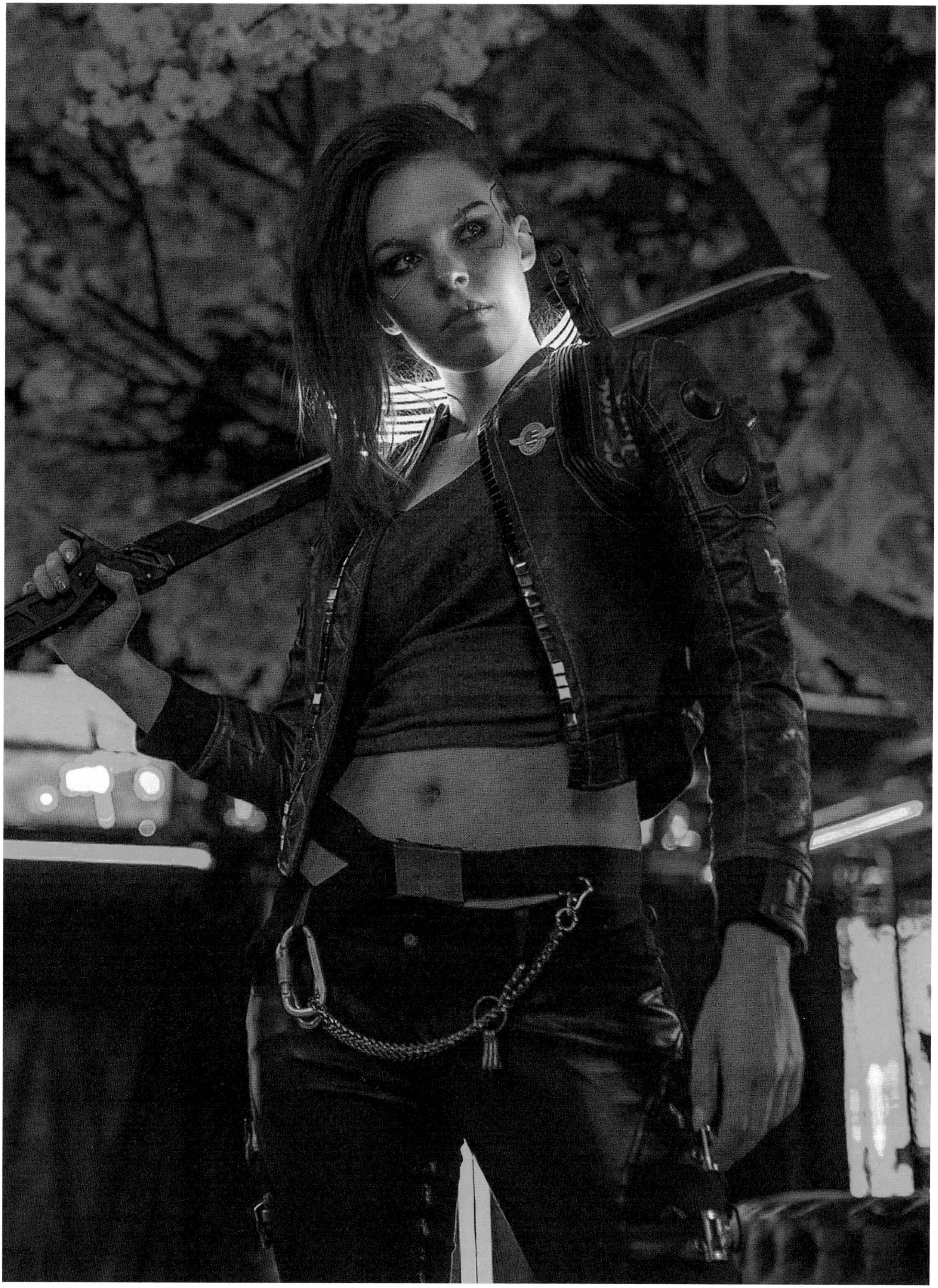

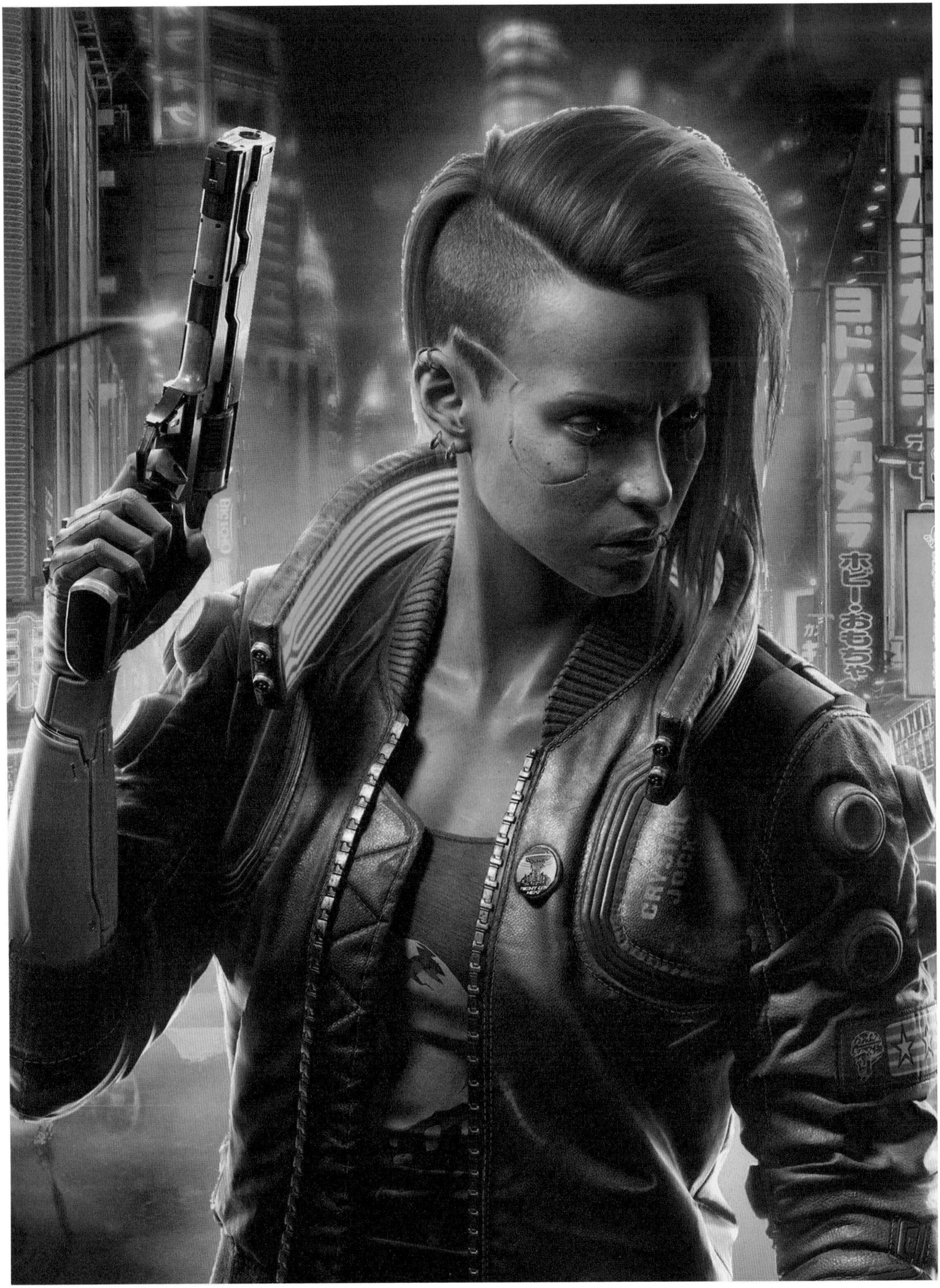

ヨドバシカメラ
ホビー・おもちゃ

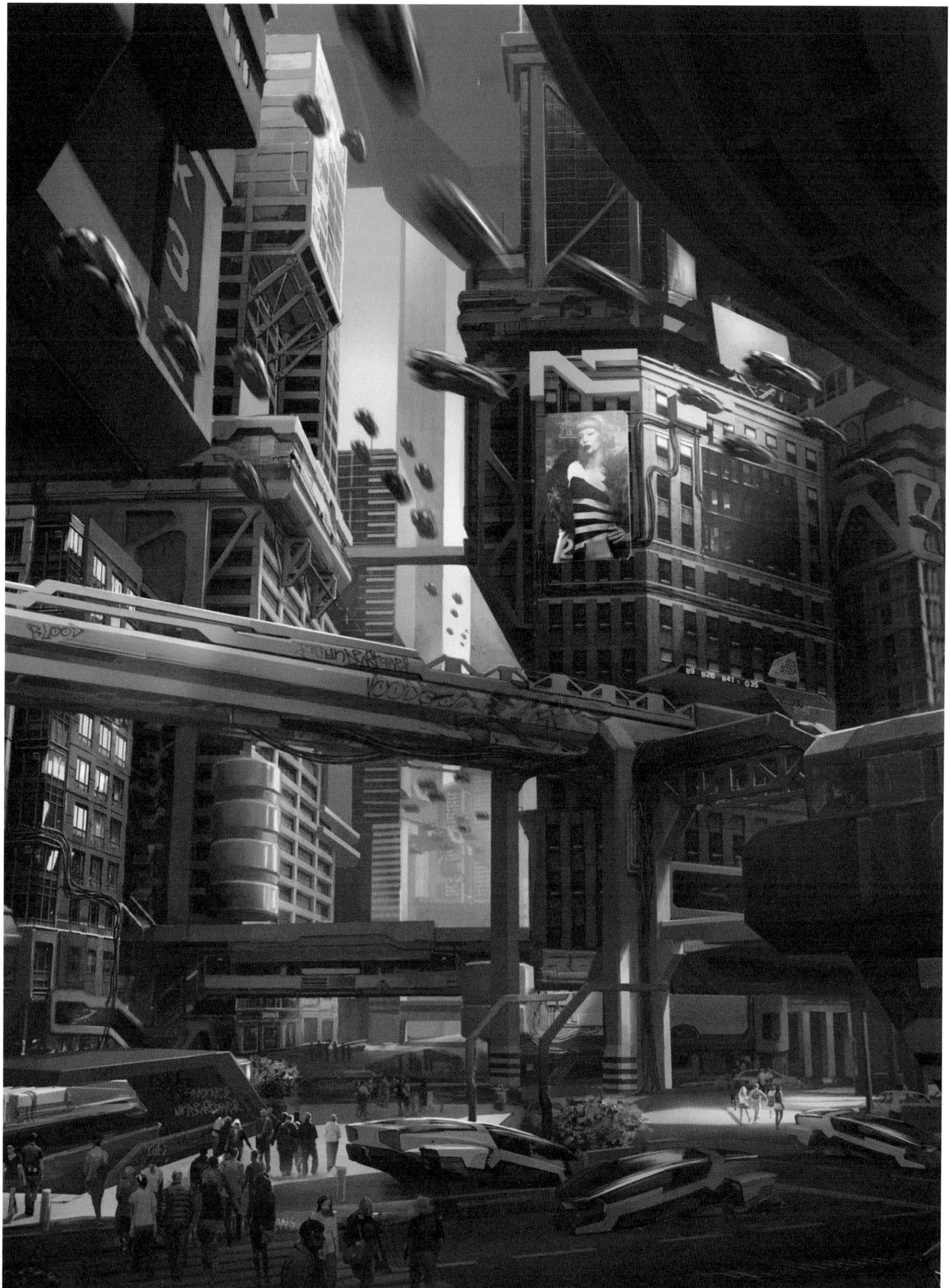

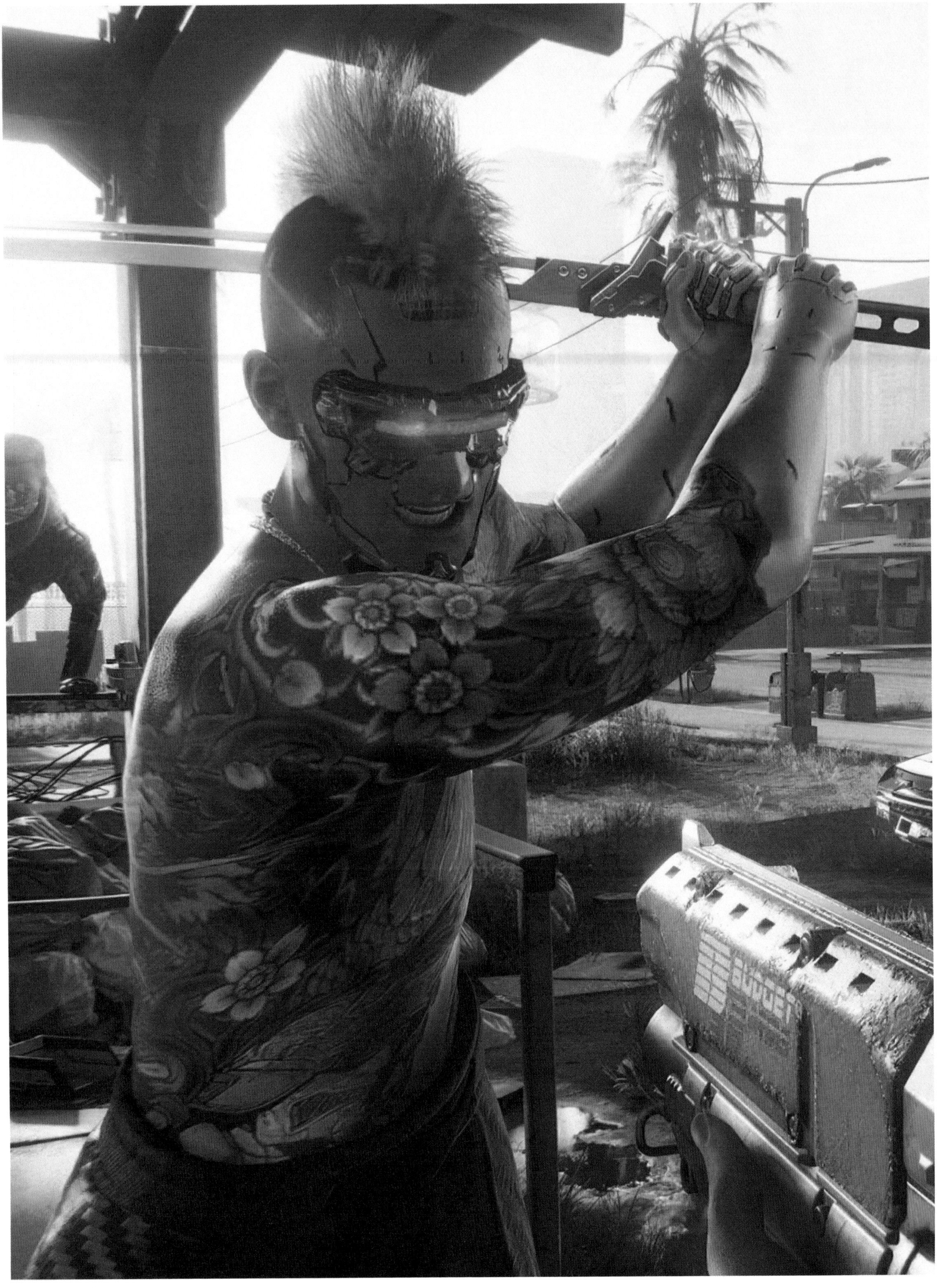
BUDGET

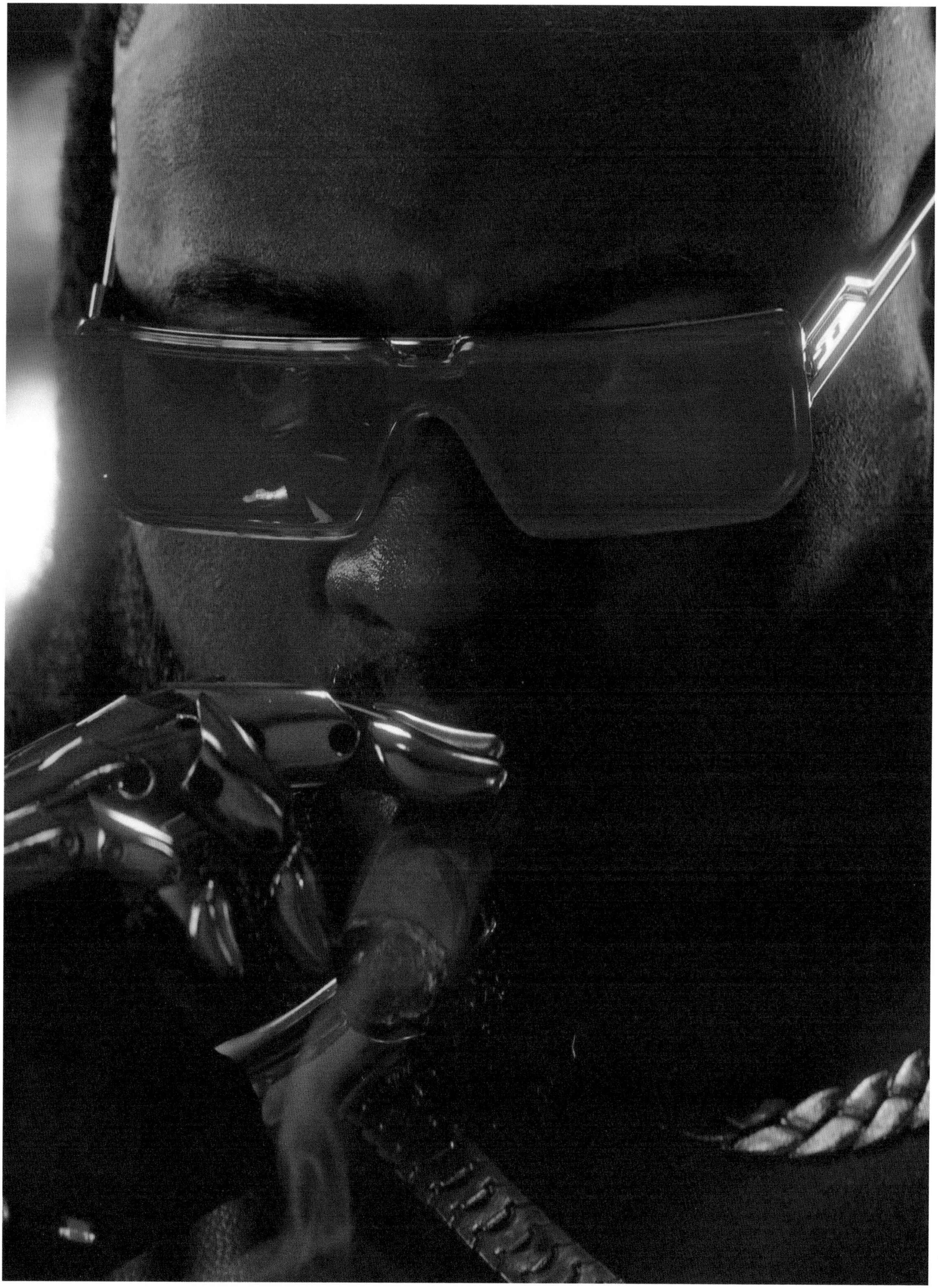

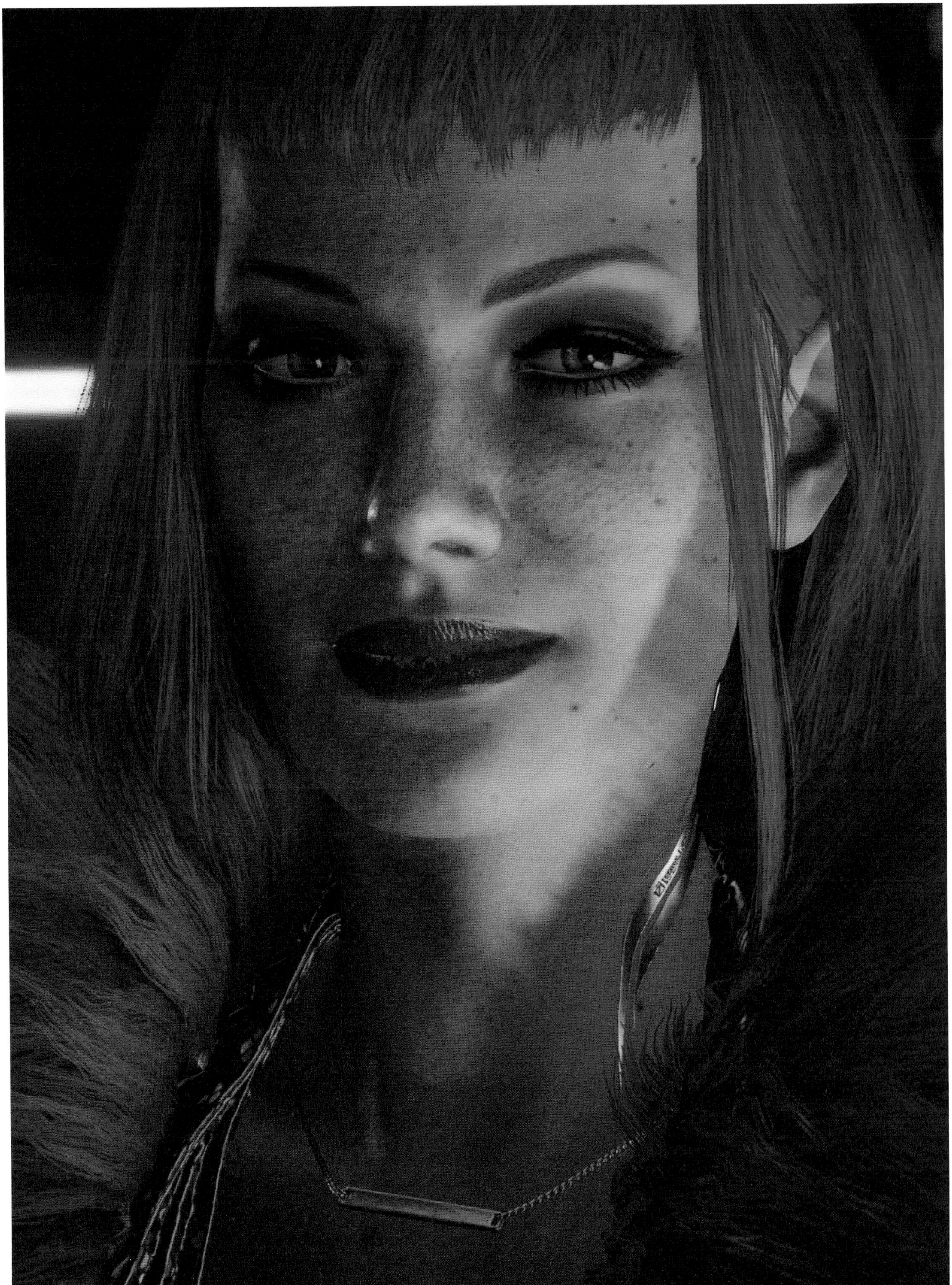

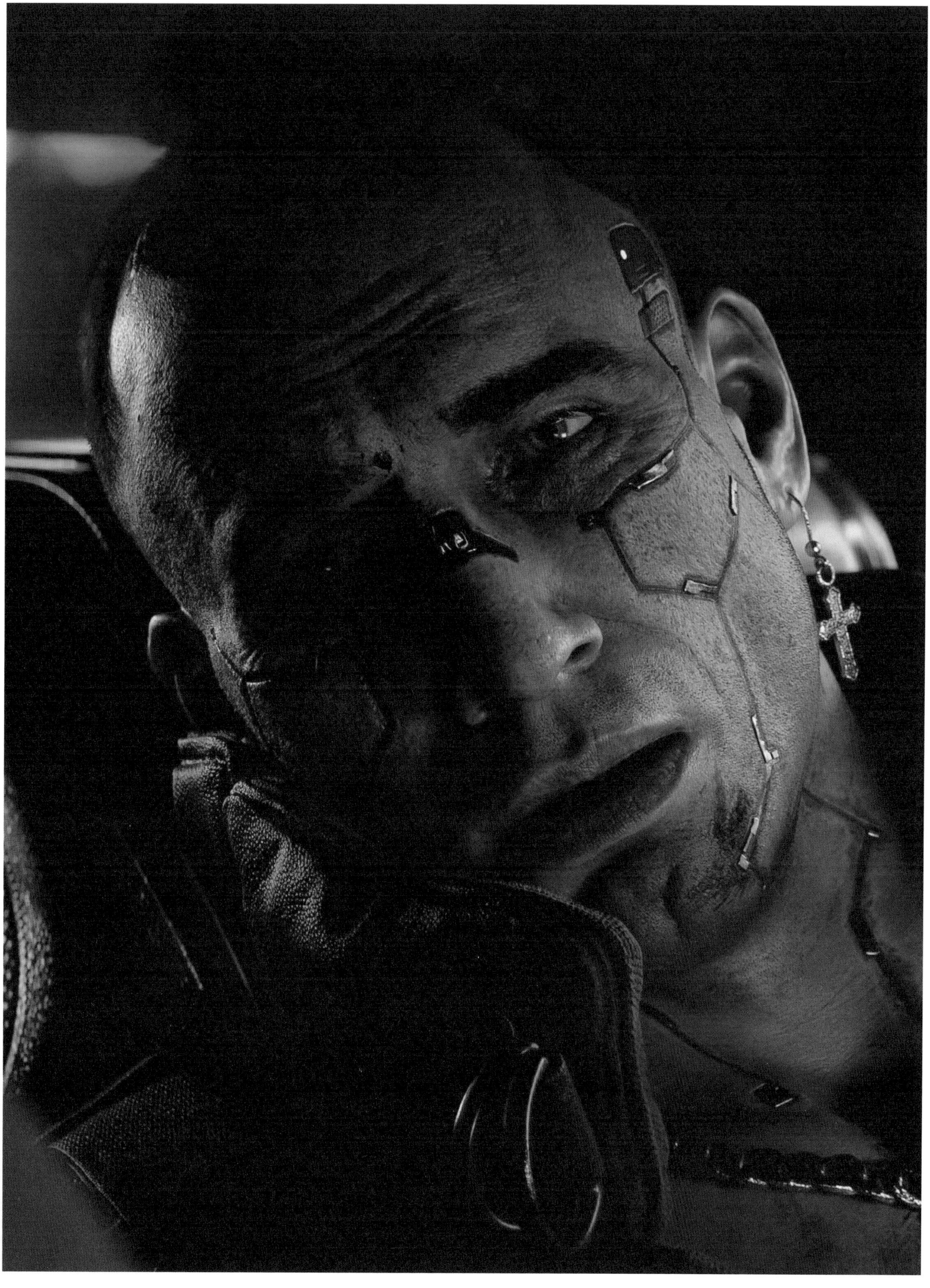

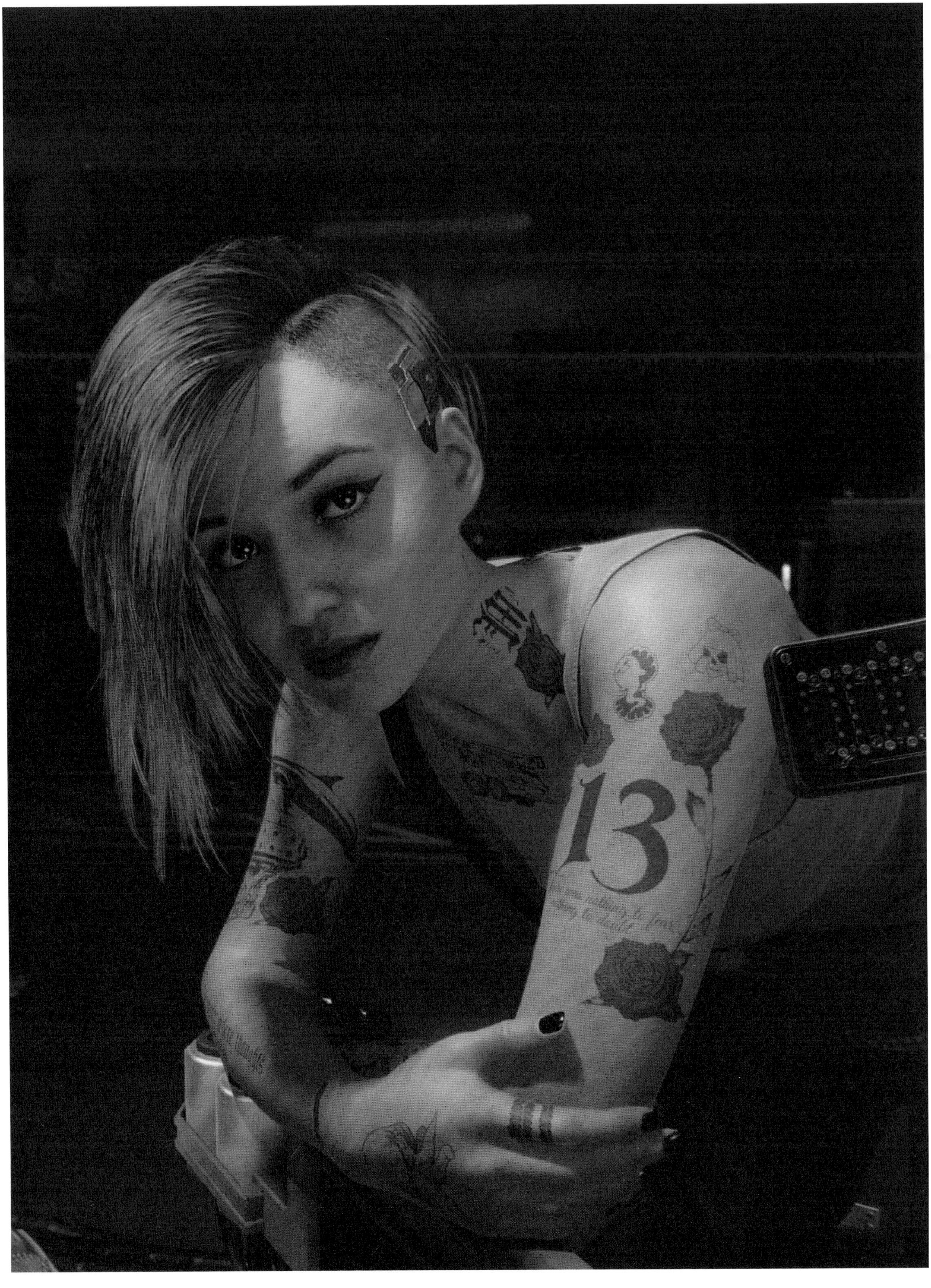

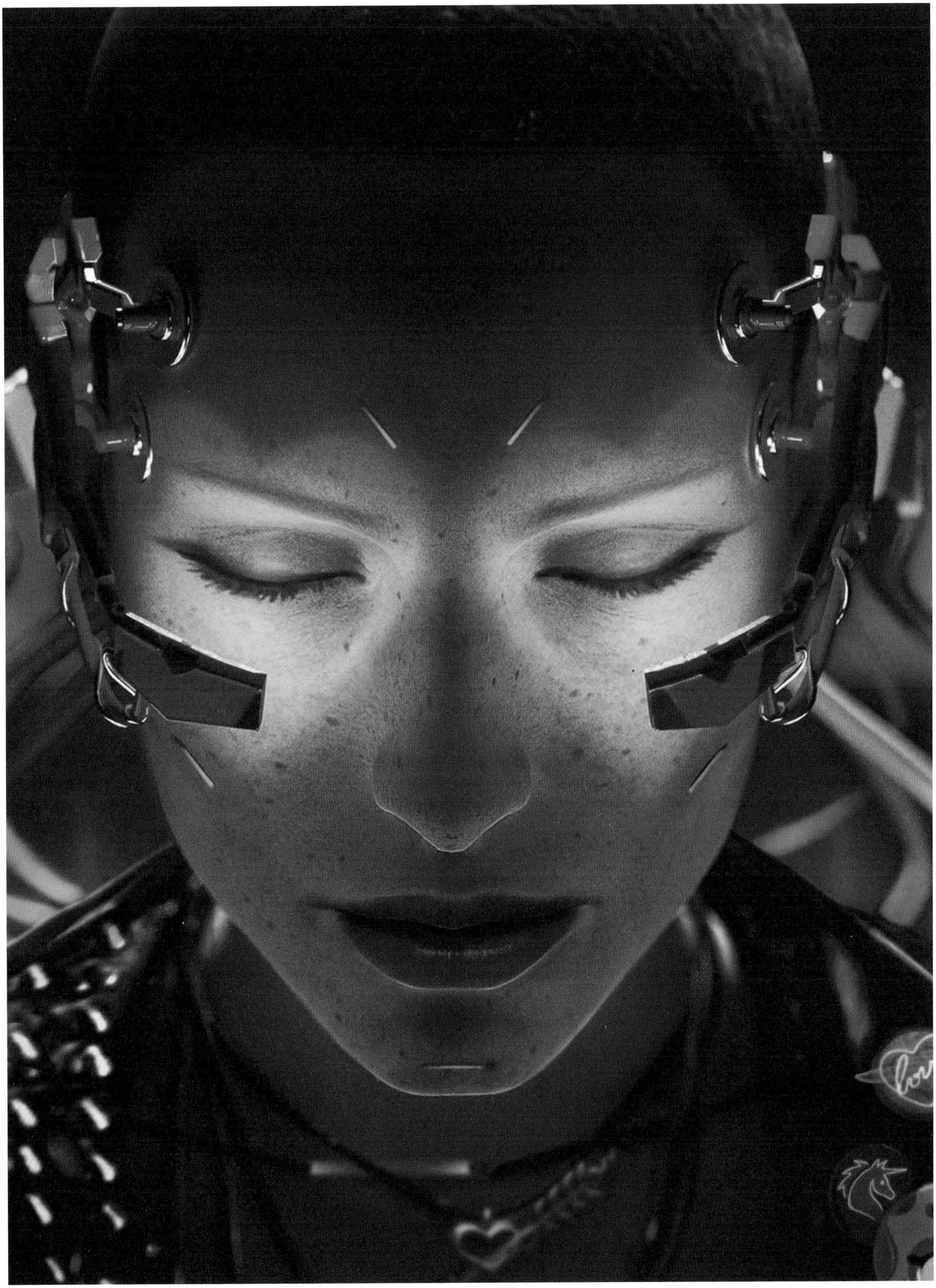

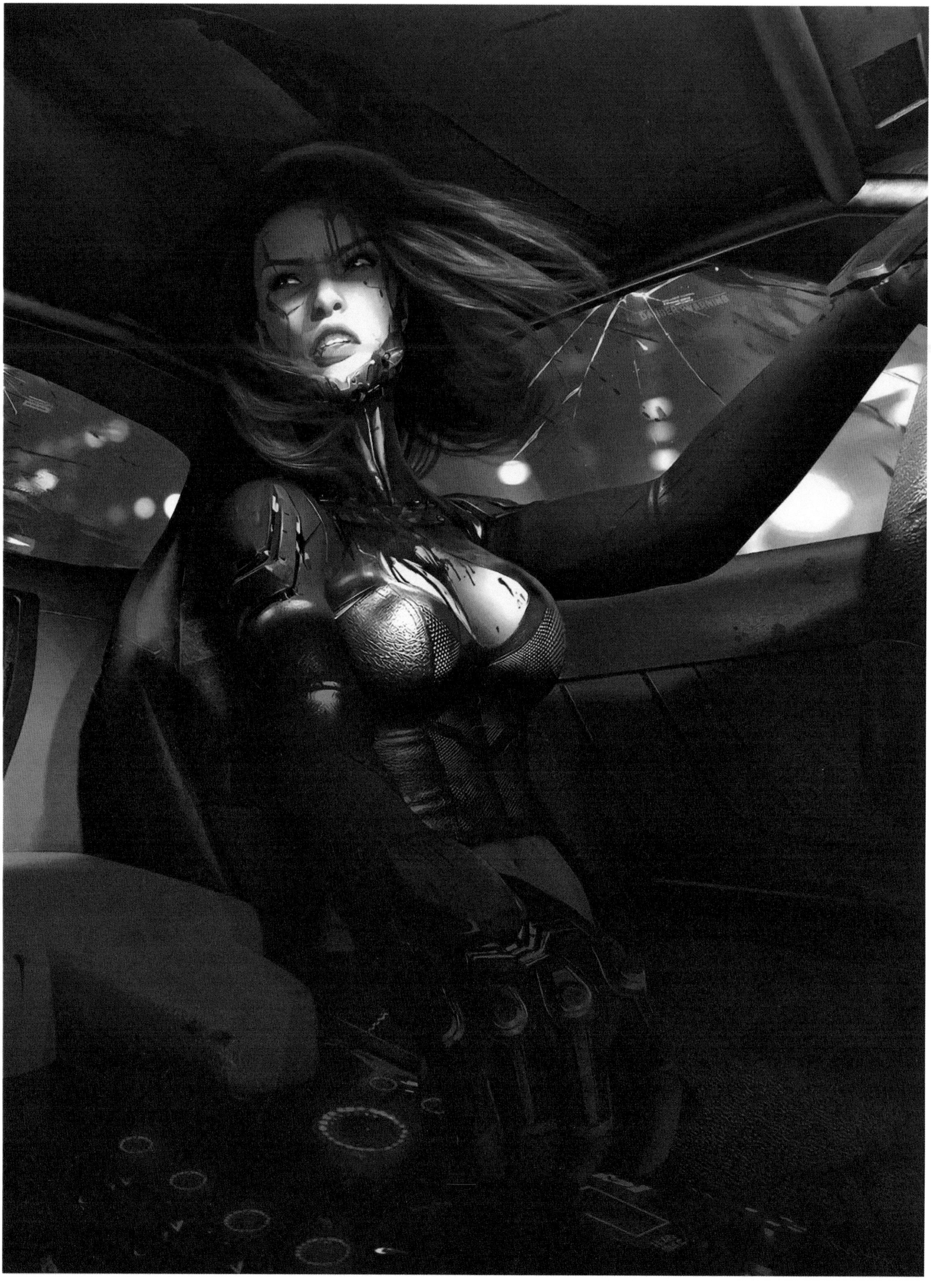

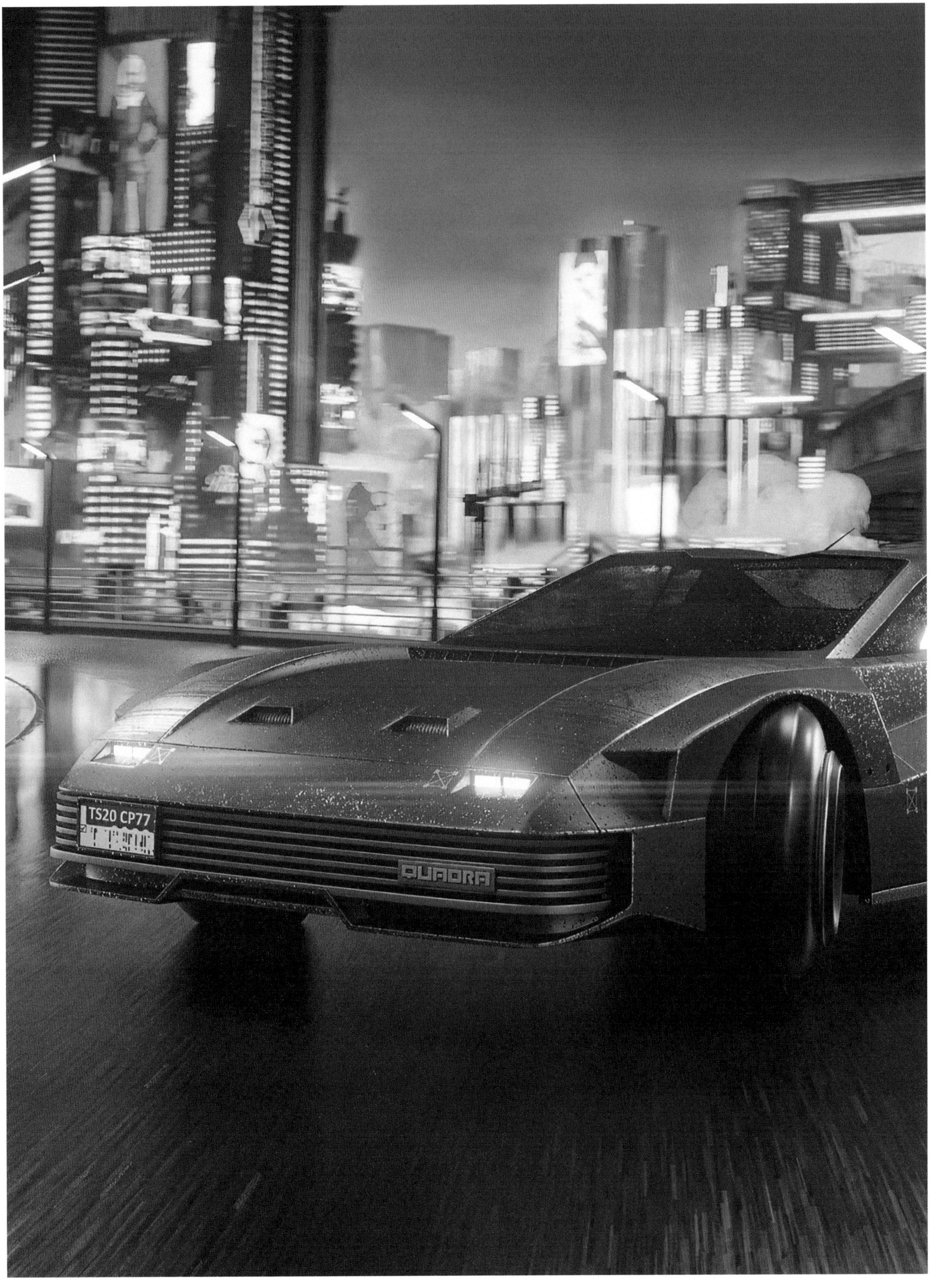
TS20 CP77
QUADRA

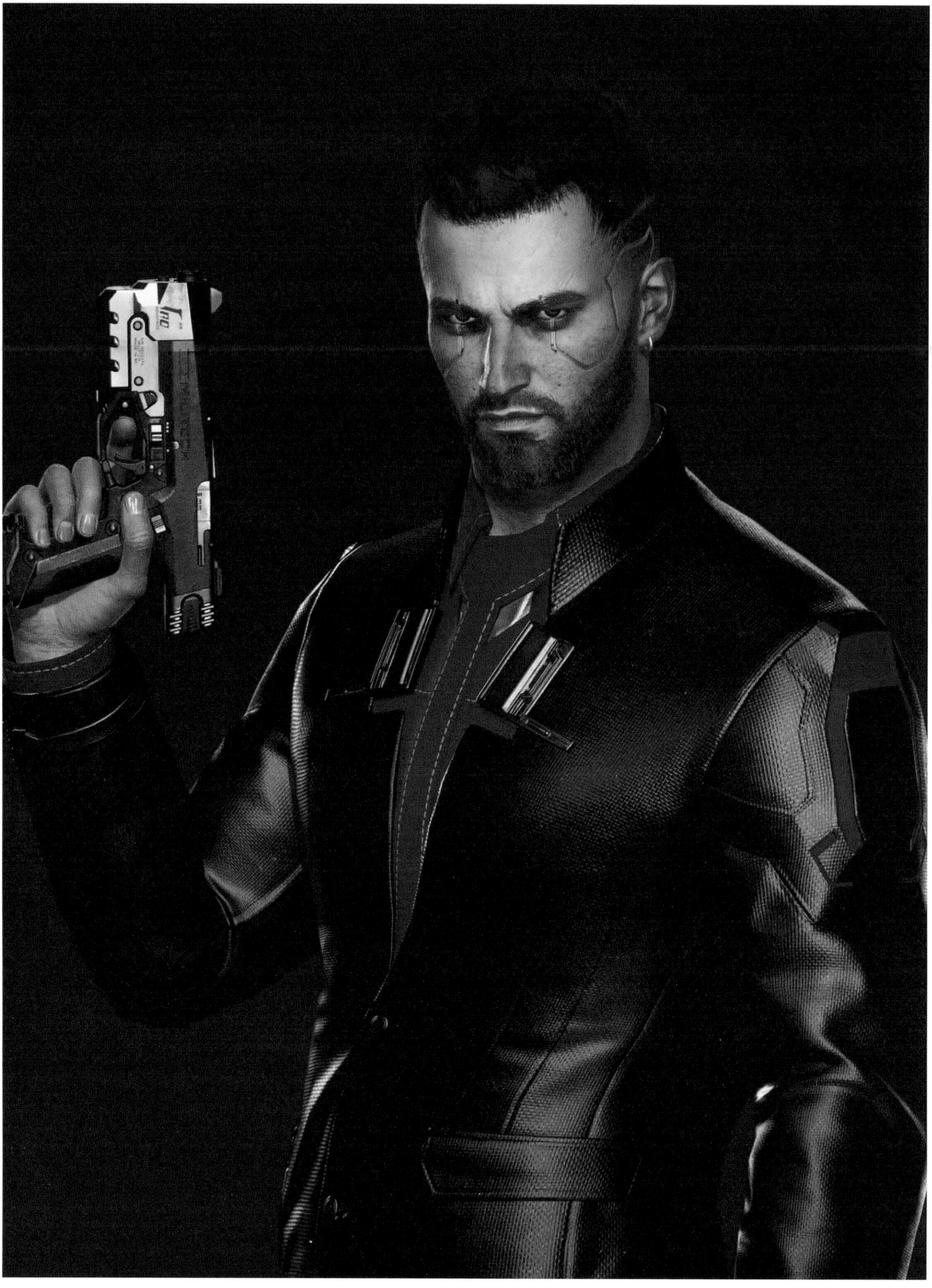

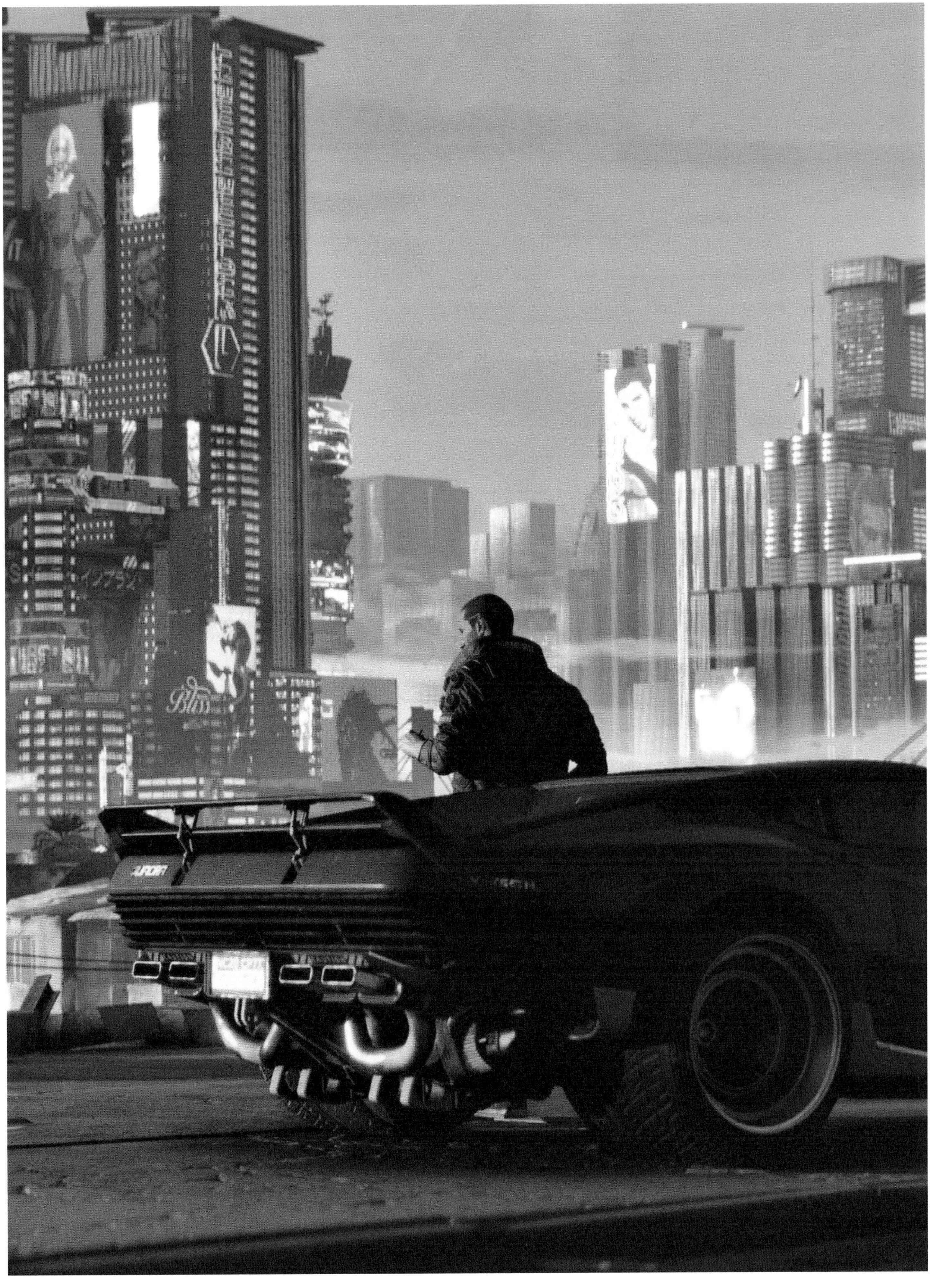
インプラン
Bliss

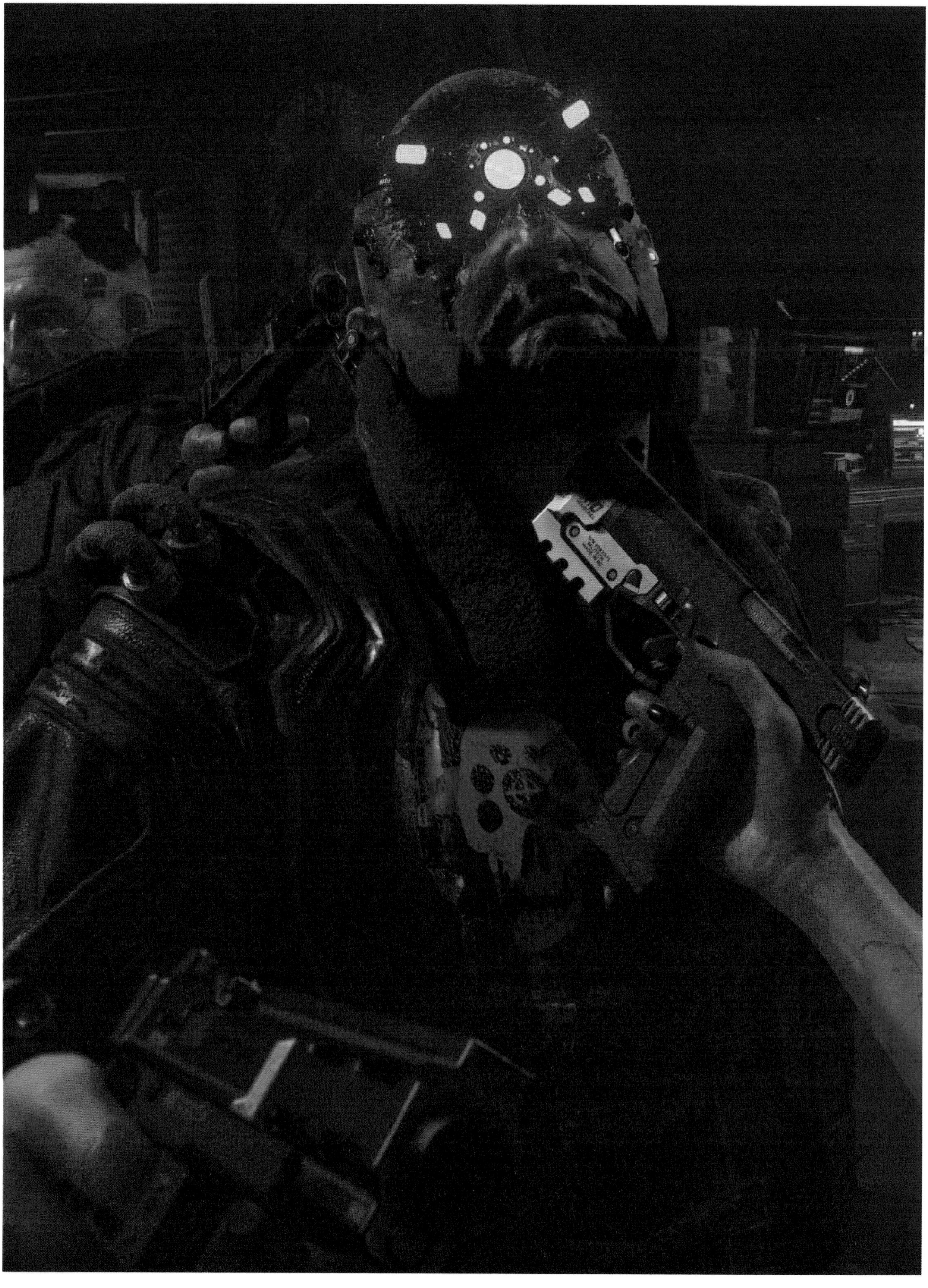

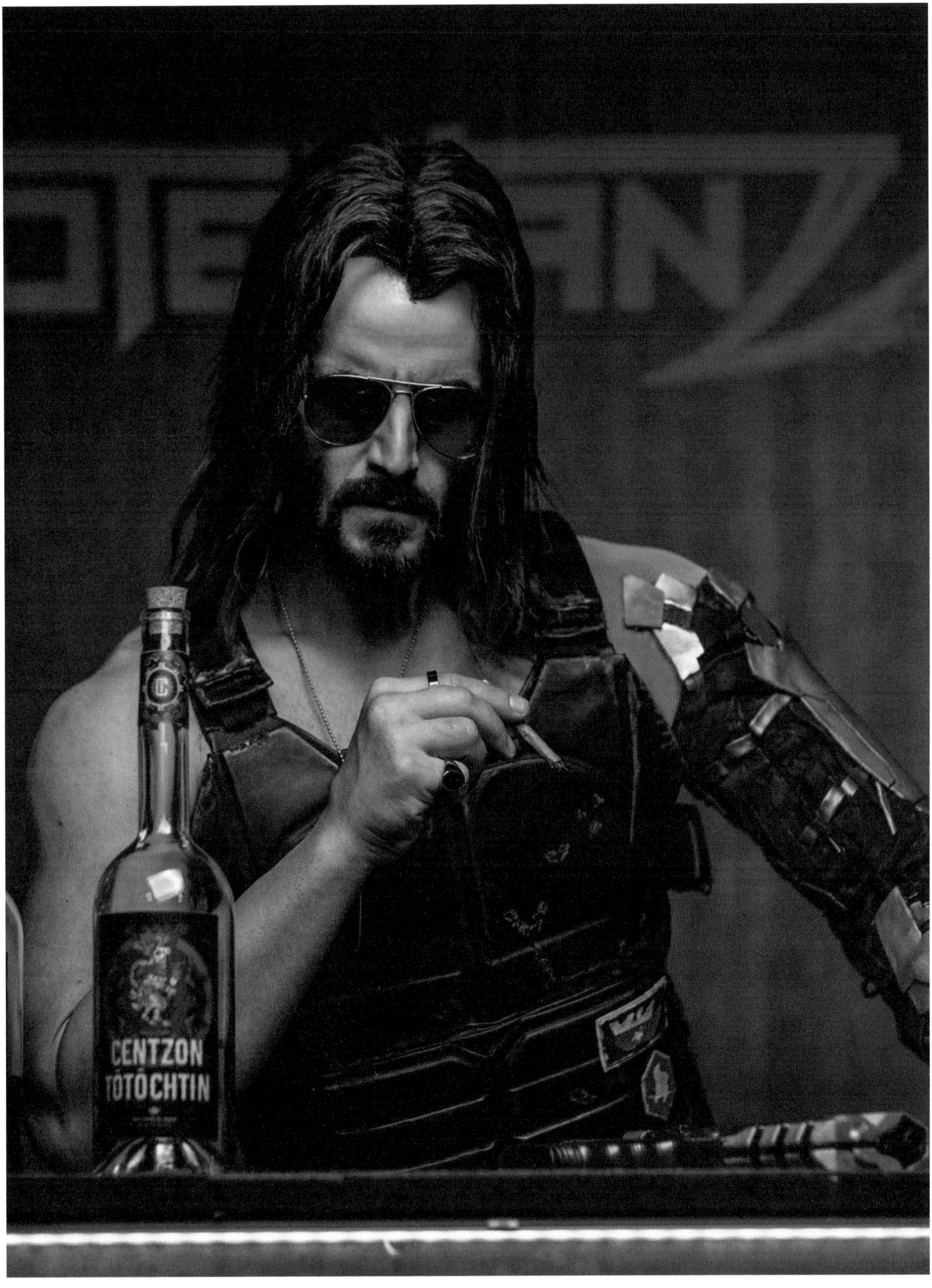
CENTZON
TOTÔCHTIN

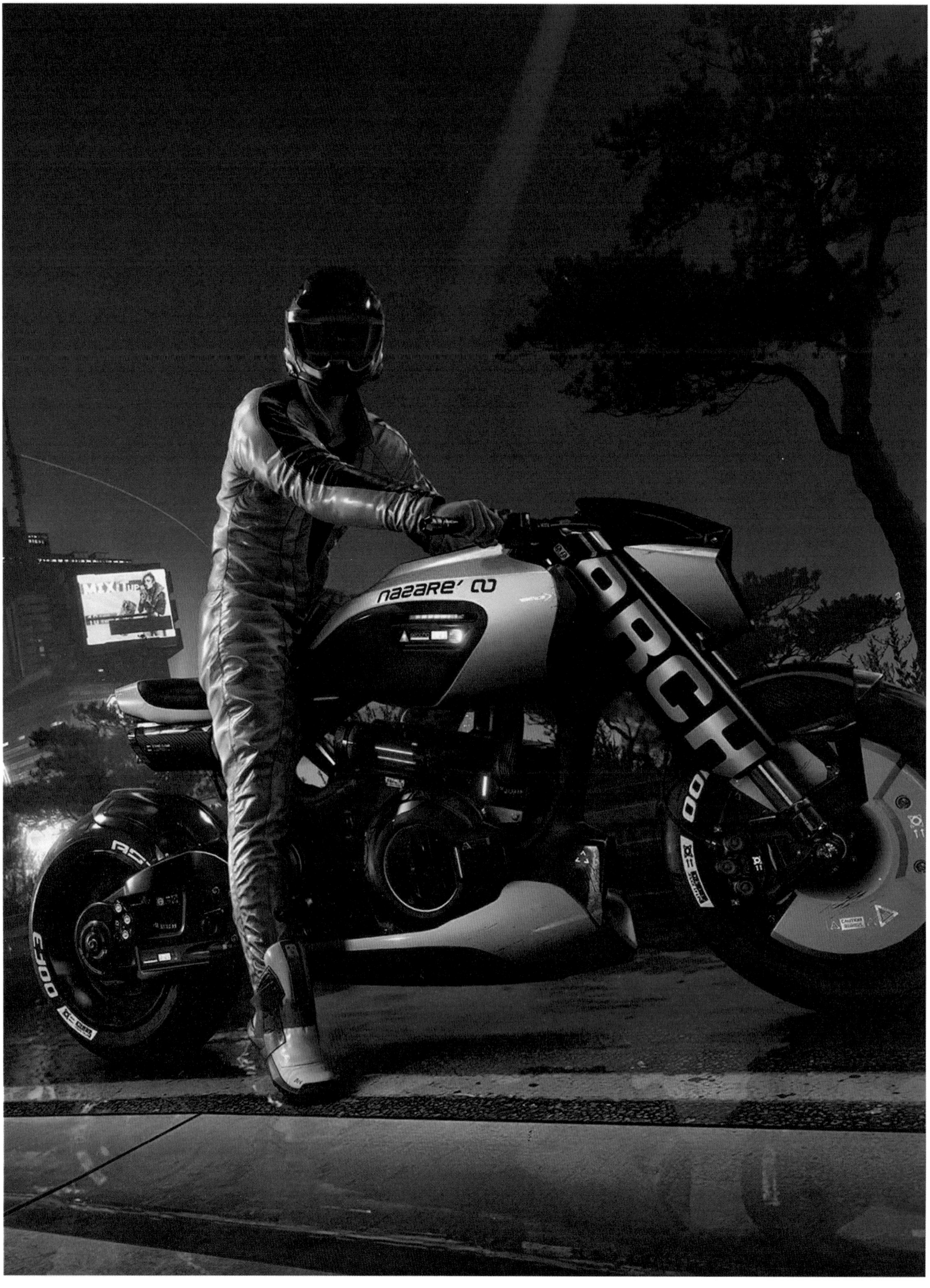
nazare'

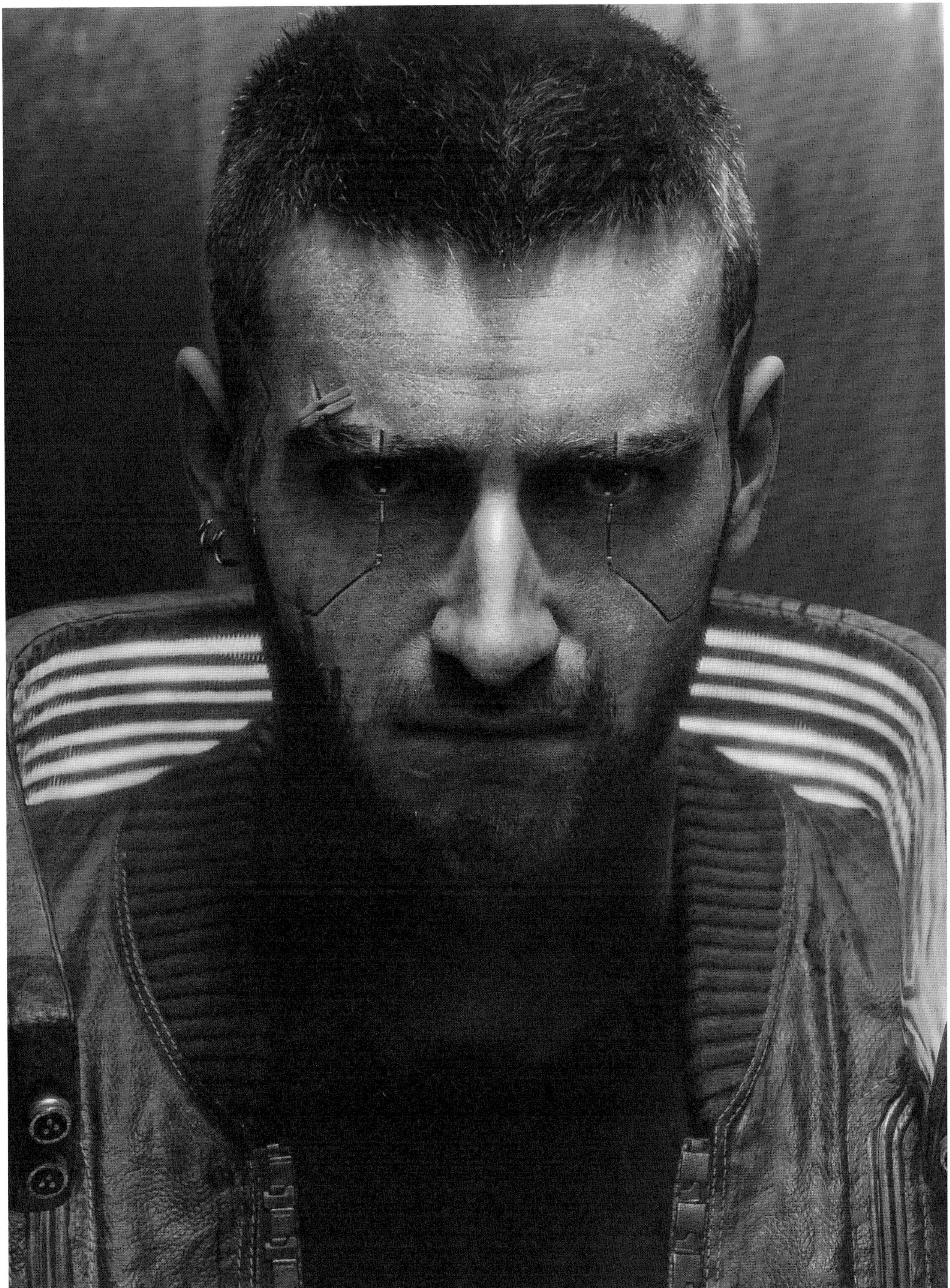

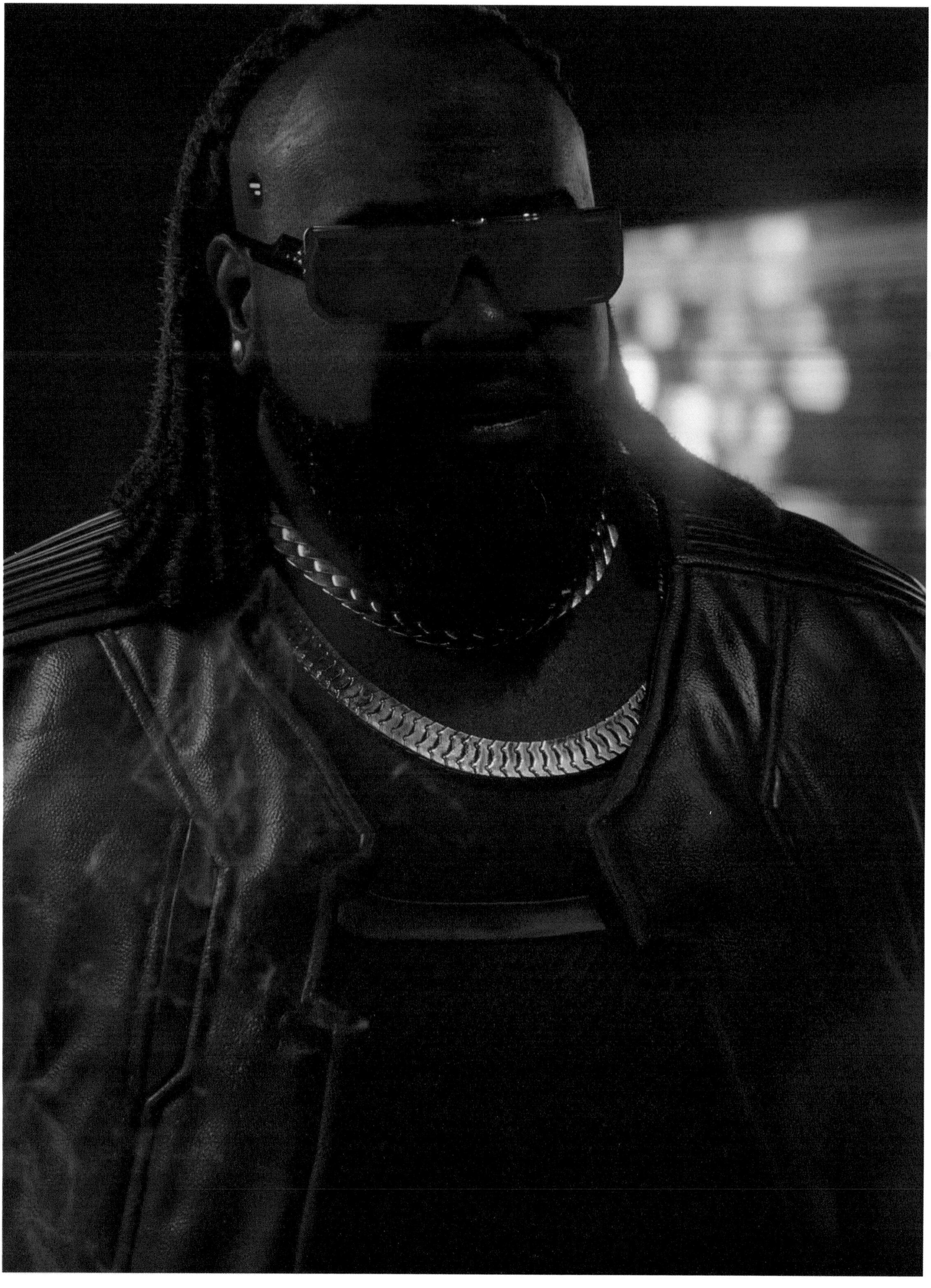

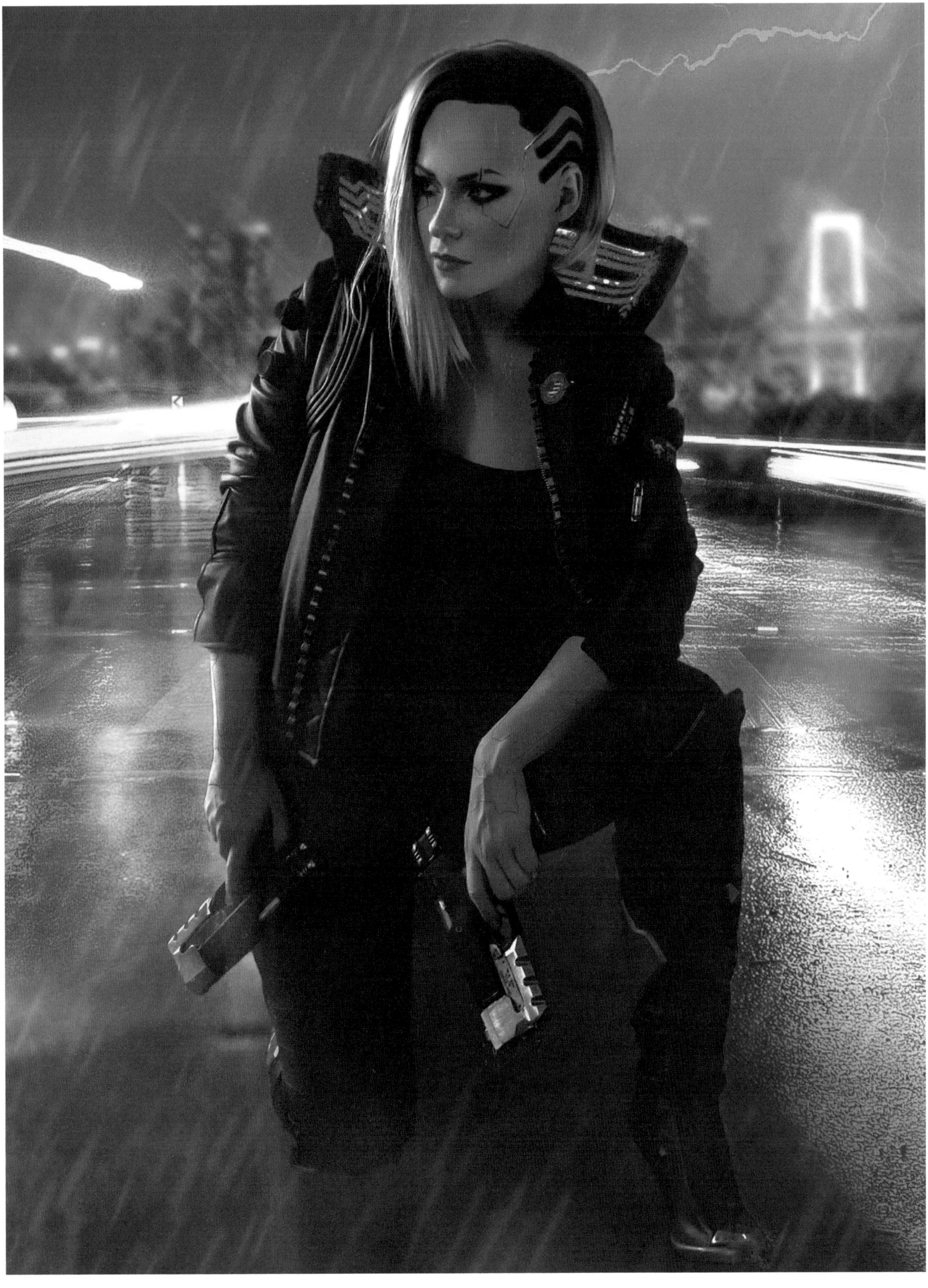

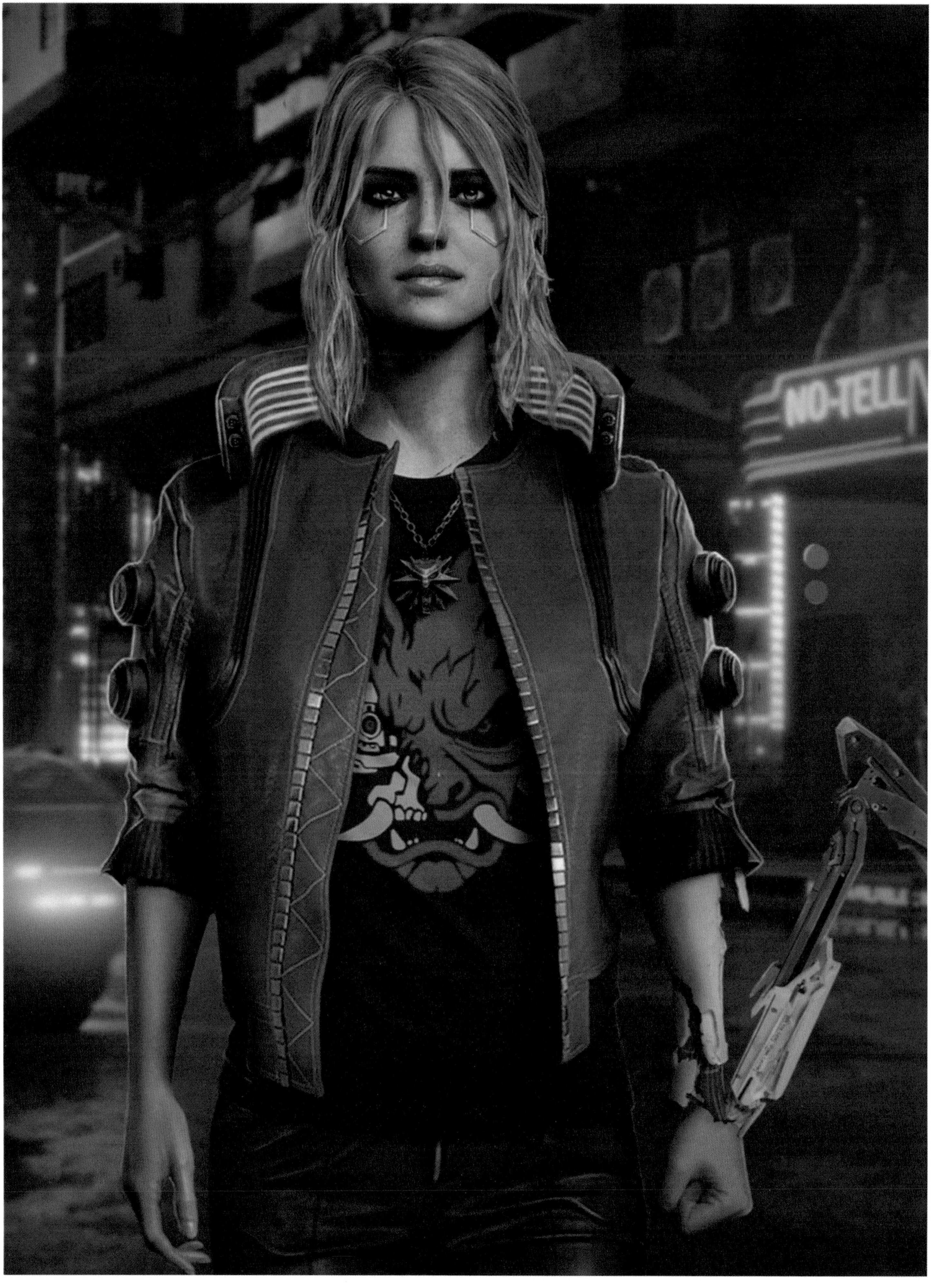
NO-TELL

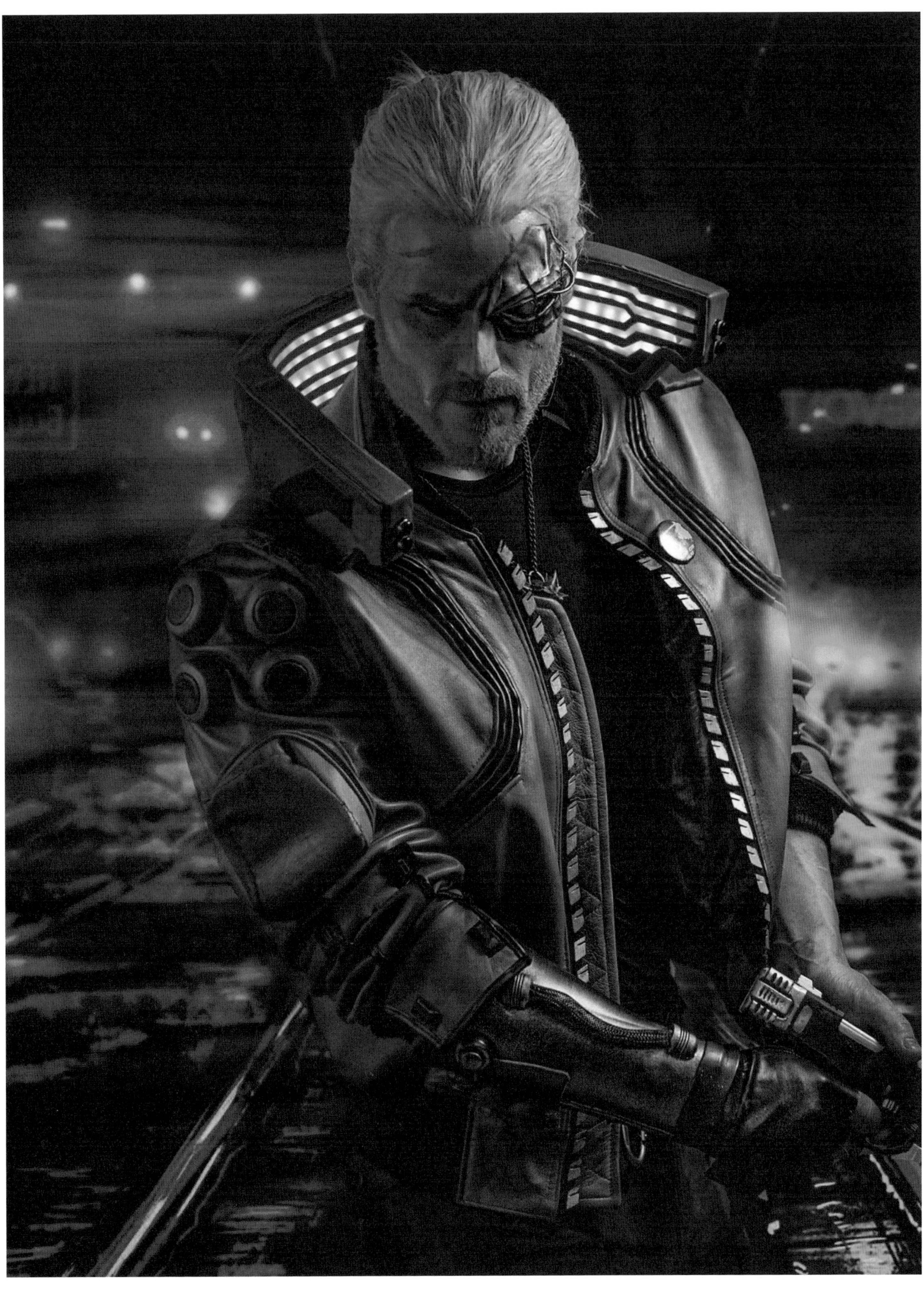

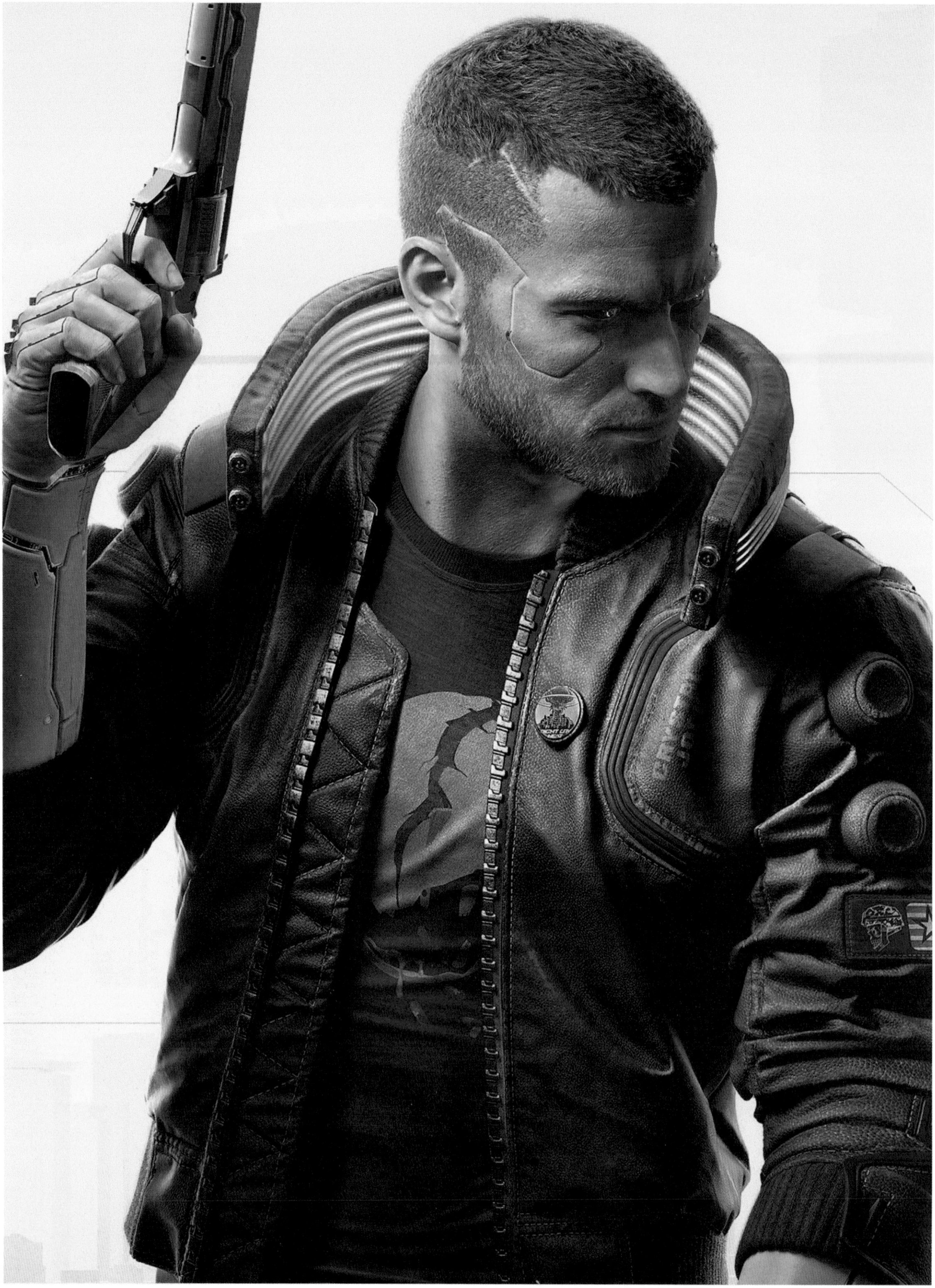

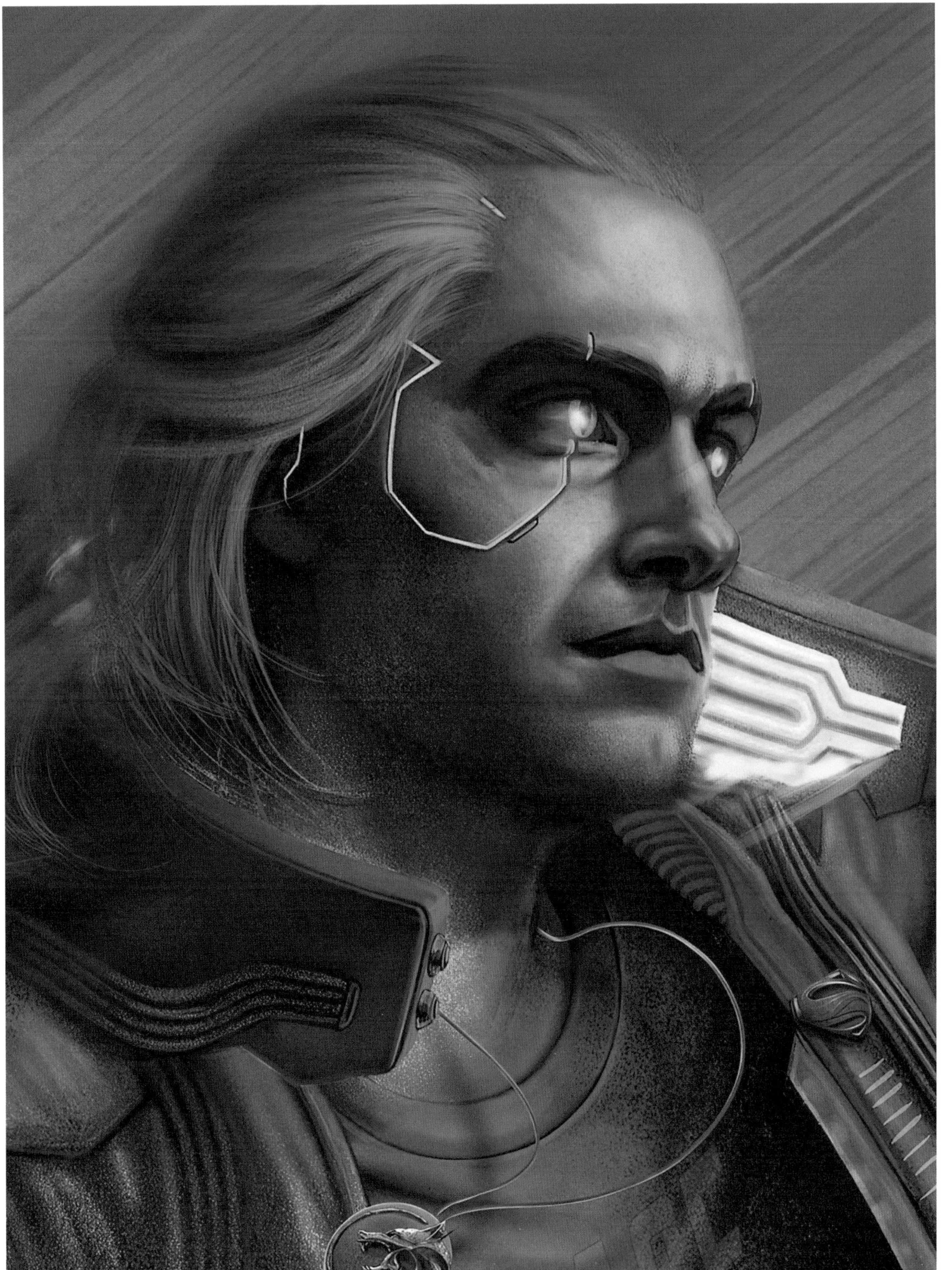

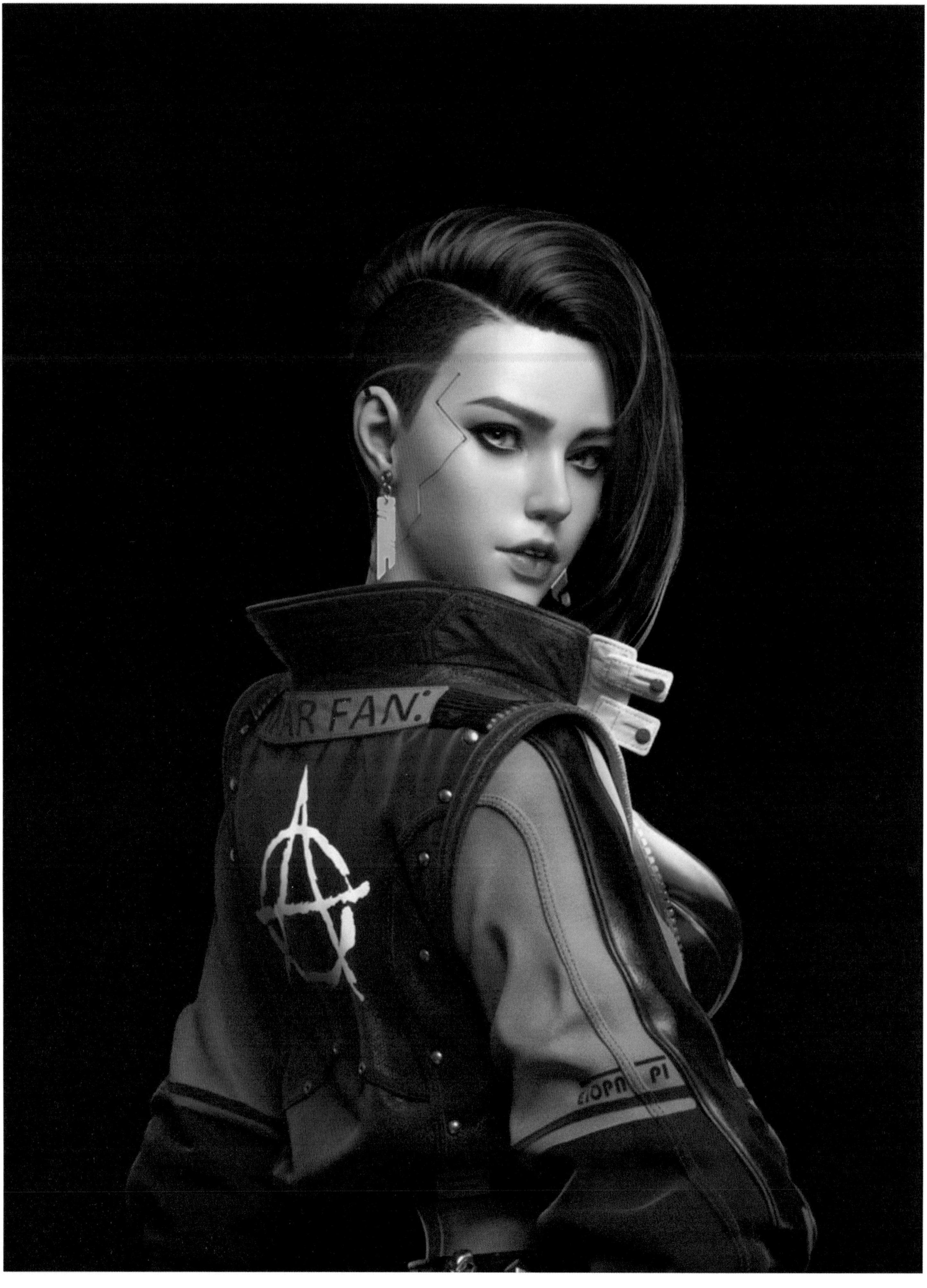
AR FAN.

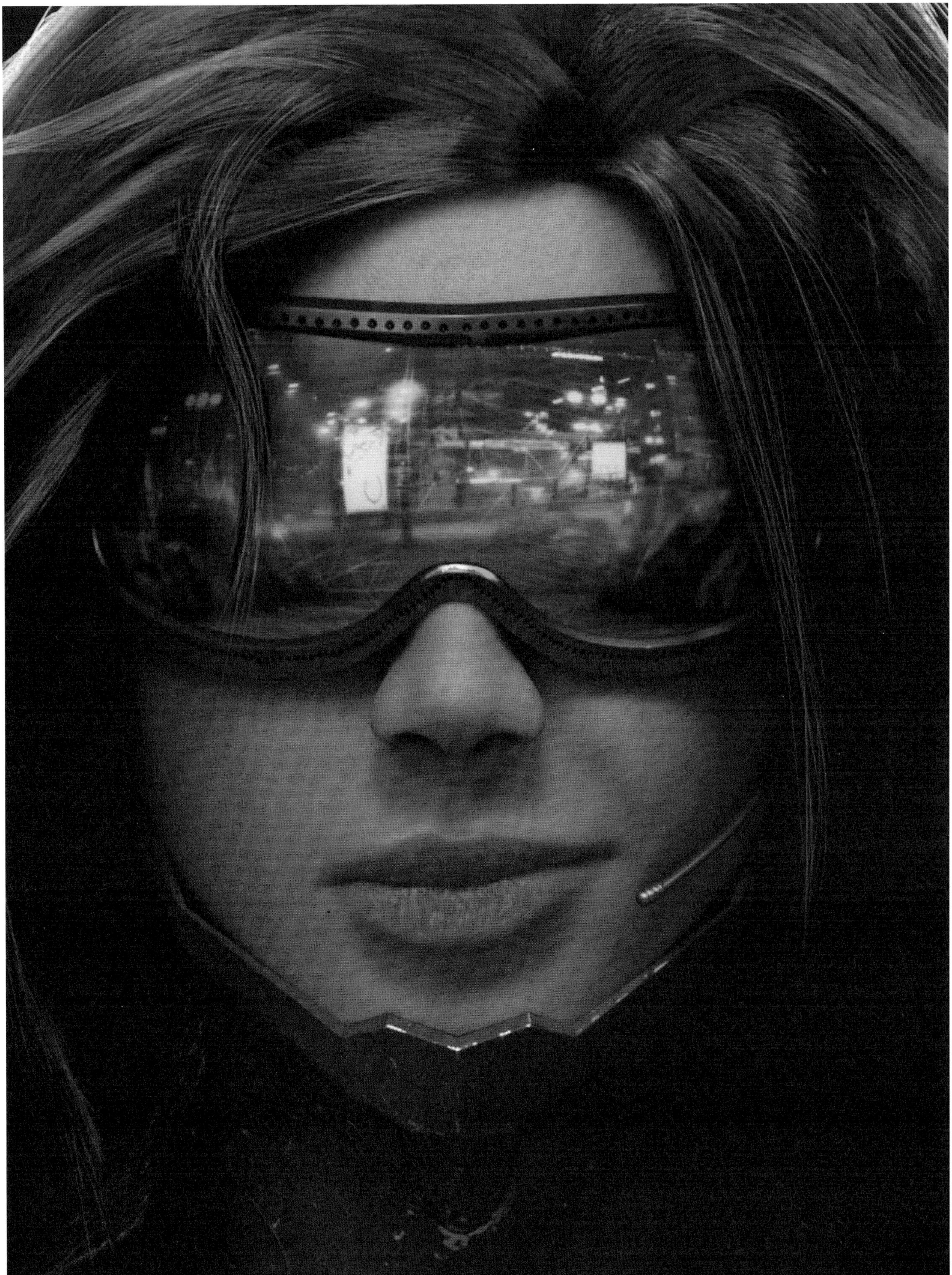

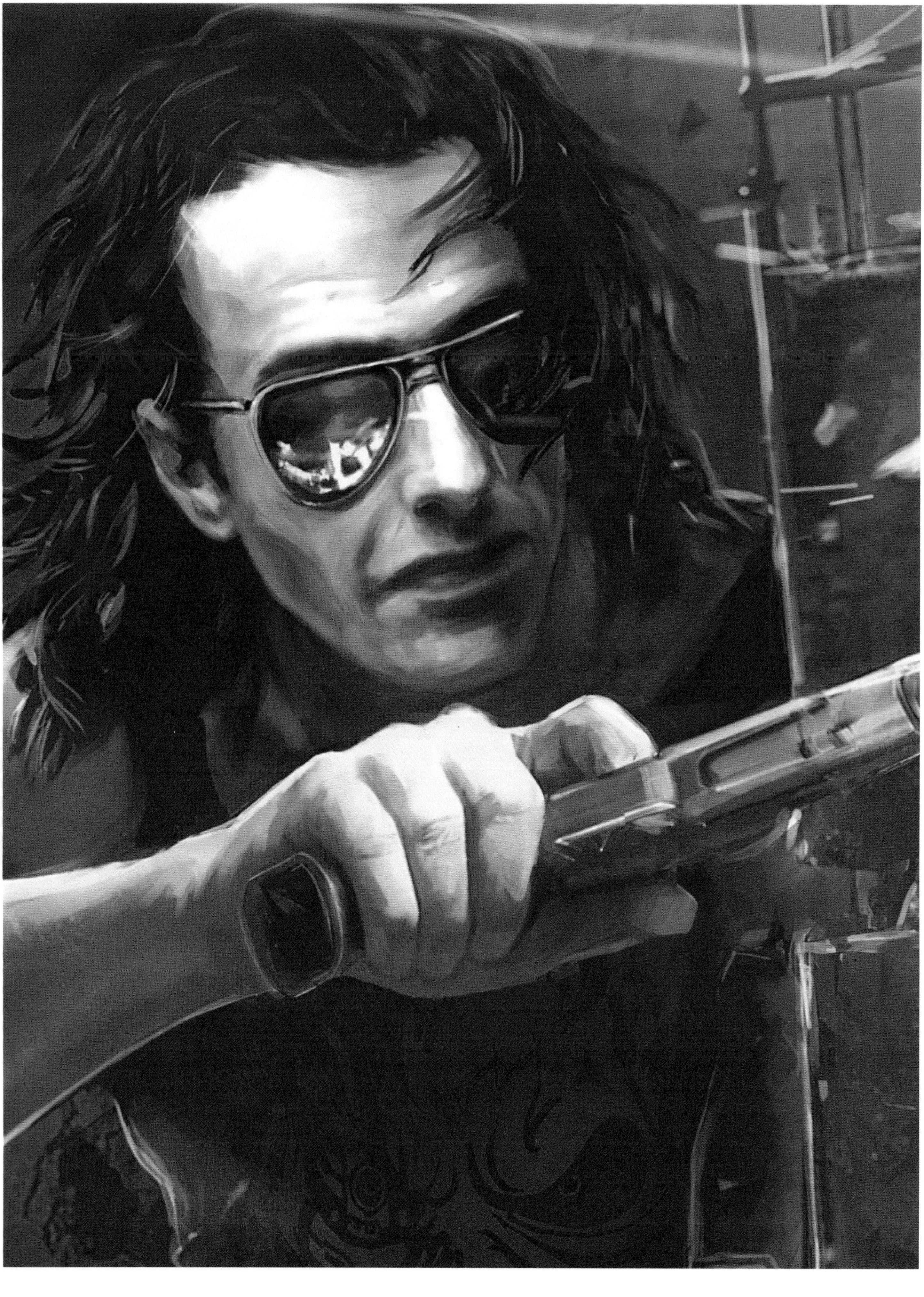

Printed in Great Britain
by Amazon

86601868R00025